Glencoe McGraw-Hill

Math Connects
Course 1

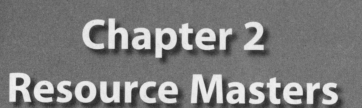

Chapter 2
Resource Masters

Consumable Workbooks Many of the worksheets contained in the Chapter Resource Masters are available as consumable workbooks in both English and Spanish.

	MHID	ISBN
Study Guide and Intervention Workbook	0-07-881032-9	978-0-07-881032-9
Skills Practice Workbook	0-07-881031-0	978-0-07-881031-2
Practice Workbook	0-07-881034-5	978-0-07-881034-3
Word Problem Practice Workbook	0-07-881033-7	978-0-07-881033-6

Spanish Versions

Study Guide and Intervention Workbook	0-07-881036-1	978-0-07-881036-7
Skills Practice Workbook	0-07-881035-3	978-0-07-881035-0
Practice Workbook	0-07-881038-8	978-0-07-881038-1
Word Problem Practice Workbook	0-07-881037-X	978-0-07-881037-4

Answers for Workbooks The answers for Chapter 2 of these workbooks can be found in the back of this Chapter Resource Masters booklet.

StudentWorks Plus™ This CD-ROM includes the entire Student Edition test along with the English workbooks listed above.

TeacherWorks Plus™ All of the materials found in this booklet are included for viewing, printing, and editing in this CD-ROM.

Spanish Assessment Masters (MHID: 0-07-881039-6, ISBN: 978-0-07-881039-8) These masters contain a Spanish version of Chapter 2 Test Form 2A and Form 2C.

McGraw Hill **Glencoe**

The McGraw·Hill Companies

Send all inquiries to:
Glencoe/McGraw-Hill
8787 Orion Place
Columbus, OH 43240

MHID: 0-07-881018-3
ISBN: 978-0-07-881018-3

Math Connects, Course 1

Printed in the United States of America.

4 5 6 7 8 9 10 REL 16 15 14 13 12 11 10

CONTENTS

Teacher's Guide to Using the
Chapter 2 Resource Masters

The *Chapter 2 Resource Masters* includes the core materials needed for Chapter 2. These materials include worksheets, extensions, and assessment options. The answers for these pages appear at the back of this booklet.

All of the materials found in this booklet are included for viewing and printing on the *TeacherWorks Plus*™ CD-ROM.

Chapter Resources

Student-Built Glossary (pages 1–2) These masters are a student study tool that presents up to twenty of the key vocabulary terms from the chapter. Students are to record definitions and/or examples for each term. You may suggest that students highlight or star the terms with which they are not familiar. Give this to students before beginning Lesson 2-1. Encourage them to add these pages to their mathematics study notebooks. Remind them to complete the appropriate words as they study each lesson.

Family Letter and Family Activity (pages 3–6) The letter informs your students' families of the mathematics they will be learning in this chapter. The family activity helps them to practice problems that are similar to those on the state test. A full solution for each problem is included. Spanish versions of these pages are also included. Give these to students to take home before beginning the chapter.

Anticipation Guide (pages 7–8) This master, presented in both English and Spanish, is a survey used before beginning the chapter to pinpoint what students may or may not know about the concepts in the chapter. Students will revisit this survey after they complete the chapter to see if their perceptions have changed.

Lesson Resources

Lesson Reading Guide Get Ready for the Lesson reiterates the questions from the beginning of the Student Edition lesson. Read the Lesson asks students to interpret the context of and relationships among terms in the lesson. Finally, Remember What You Learned asks students to summarize what they have learned using various representation techniques. Use as a study tool for note taking or as an informal reading assignment. It is also a helpful tool for ELL (English Language Learners).

Study Guide and Intervention This master provides vocabulary, key concepts, additional worked-out examples and Check Your Progress exercises to use as a reteaching activity. It can also be used in conjunction with the Student Edition as an instructional tool for students who have been absent.

Skills Practice This master focuses more on the computational nature of the lesson. Use as an additional practice option or as homework for second-day teaching of the lesson.

Practice This master closely follows the types of problems found in the Exercises section of the Student Edition and includes word problems. Use as an additional practice option or as homework for second-day teaching of the lesson.

Word Problem Practice This master includes additional practice in solving word problems that apply the concepts of the lesson. Use as an additional practice or as homework for second-day teaching of the lesson.

Enrichment These activities may extend the concepts of the lesson, offer a historical or multicultural look at the concepts, or widen students' perspectives on the mathematics they are learning. They are written for use with all levels of students.

Graphing Calculator, Scientific Calculator, or Spreadsheet Activities These activities present ways in which technology can be used with the concepts in some lessons of this chapter. Use as an alternative approach to some concepts or as an integral part of your lesson presentation.

Assessment Options

The assessment masters in the *Chapter 2 Resource Masters* offer a wide range of assessment tools for formative (monitoring) assessment and summative (final) assessment.

Student Recording Sheet This master corresponds with the Test Practice at the end of the chapter.

Extended-Response Rubric This master provides information for teachers and students on how to assess performance on open-ended questions.

Quizzes Four free-response quizzes offer assessment at appropriate intervals in the chapter.

Mid-Chapter Test This 1-page test provides an option to assess the first half of the chapter. It parallels the timing of the Mid-Chapter Quiz in the Student Edition and includes both multiple-choice and free-response questions.

Vocabulary Test This test is suitable for all students. It includes a list of vocabulary words and 10 questions to assess students' knowledge of those words. This can also be used in conjunction with one of the leveled chapter tests.

Leveled Chapter Tests

- *Form 1* contains multiple-choice questions and is intended for use with below grade level students.

- *Forms 2A and 2B* contain multiple-choice questions aimed at on grade level students. These tests are similar in format to offer comparable testing situations.

- *Forms 2C and 2D* contain free-response questions aimed at on grade level students. These tests are similar in format to offer comparable testing situations.

- *Form 3* is a free-response test for use with above grade level students.

All of the above mentioned tests include a free-response Bonus question.

Extended-Response Test Performance assessment tasks are suitable for all students. Samples answers and a scoring rubric are included for evaluation.

Standardized Test Practice These three pages are cumulative in nature. It includes two parts: multiple-choice questions with bubble-in answer format and short-answer free-response questions.

Answers

- The answers for the Anticipation Guide and Lesson Resources are provided as reduced pages with answers appearing in red.

- Full-size answer keys are provided for the assessment masters.

2 Student-Built Glossary

This is an alphabetical list of new vocabulary terms you will learn in Chapter 2. As you study the chapter, complete each term's definition or description. Remember to add the page number where you found the term. Add this page to your math study notebook to review vocabulary at the end of the chapter.

Vocabulary Term	Found on Page	Definition/Description/Example
average		
bar graph		
data		
frequency		
graph		
horizontal axis		
integers		
interval		
key		
leaves		
line graph		

2   Student-Built Glossary   *(continued)*

Vocabulary Term	Found on Page	Definition/Description/Example
line plot		
mean		
measures of central tendency		
median		
mode		
negative numbers		
opposites		
outlier		
positive numbers		
range		
scale		
stem-and-leaf plot		
stems		
vertical axis		

2 Family Letter

Dear Parent or Guardian:

We use math in many of our daily routines. One of the things we try to do in this class is relate activities in the classroom to activities in the real world. Making this connection will help students realize the importance of learning math concepts.

In **Chapter 2, Statistics and Graphs**, your child will be learning about bar graphs, line graphs, stem-and-leaf plots, line plots, mean, median, mode, range, selecting appropriate displays, and integers in the context of graphing. In the study of this chapter, your child will complete a variety of daily classroom assignments and activities and possibly produce a chapter project.

By signing this letter and returning it with your child, you agree to encourage your child by getting involved. Enclosed is an activity that you can do with your child that practices how the math we will be learning in Chapter 2 might be tested. You may also wish to log on to **glencoe.com** for self-check quizzes and other study help. If you have any questions or comments, feel free to contact me at school.

Sincerely,

Signature of Parent or Guardian _____ Date _____

2 Family Activity

State Test Practice

Fold the page along the dashed line. Work each problem on another piece of paper. Then unfold the page to check your work.

1. Use the data on the table below to calculate the mean, median, mode, and range of the ages of people who worked at Whetstone Middle School's Spring Festival.

12	15	14	39	45	15
71	13	67	11	14	13
55	54	12	14	15	10
33	15	12	51	25	23

Which selection includes all of the correct answers?

A mean = 27; median = 15; modes = 12 and 14; range = 81

B mean = 28; median = 15; modes = 12 and 14; range = 61

C mean = 27; median = 15; mode = 15; range = 61

D mean = 27; median = 15; modes = 12 and 14; range = 61

2. Refer to the table below. During which month were U.S. citizens least likely to be unemployed?

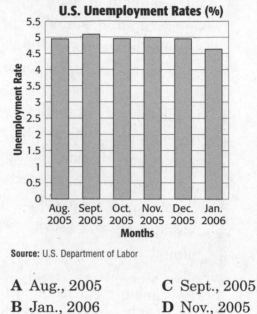

U.S. Unemployment Rates (%)

Source: U.S. Department of Labor

A Aug., 2005   C Sept., 2005

B Jan., 2006   D Nov., 2005

Fold here.

- -

Solution

1. *Hint: It is always best to sort a large set of numbers from least to greatest when finding mean, median, mode, and range.*

   To find the mean, add all the numbers then divide by how many numbers are in the set. There are 24 numbers, and the sum is 648. The mean is 648 ÷ 24 or 27. This eliminates choice B. You need not calculate the median since all answer choices have the same value. The mode is the number or numbers that occur(s) most often in the set. In this set, 15 occurs most often. Only choice C has a mean of 27 and a mode of 15.

Solution

2. U.S. Citizens are least likely to be unemployed when the employment rate is lowest, which corresponds with the shortest bar on the graph above. The shortest bar occurs in January, so that is when citizens are least likely to be unemployed.

The answer is **C**.

The answer is **B**.

2 Carta a la familia

Estimado padre o apoderado:

Usamos las matemáticas en diversas rutinas diarias. Una de las cosas que tratamos de lograr en esta clase es relacionar las actividades del aula con las del mundo real para ayudar a los alumnos a darse cuenta de la importancia del aprendizaje de conceptos matemáticos.

En el **Capítulo 2, Estadísticas y gráficas**, su hijo(a) aprenderá sobre gráficas de barras, gráficas lineales, gráficas de tallo y hojas, esquemas lineales, la media, la mediana, la moda, el rango, la selección de despliegues adecuados y enteros en cuanto a gráficas. En el estudio de este capítulo, su hijo(a) completará una variedad de tareas y actividades diarias y es posible que trabaje en un proyecto del capítulo.

Al firmar esta carta y devolverla con su hijo(a), usted se compromete a ayudarlo(a) a participar en su aprendizaje. Junto con esta carta, va incluida una actividad que puede realizar con él(ella) y la cual practica lo que podrían encontrar en las pruebas de los conceptos matemáticos que aprenderán en el Capítulo 2. Además, visiten **glencoe.com** para ver autocontroles y otras ayudas para el estudio. Si tiene cualquier pregunta o comentario, por favor contácteme en la escuela.

Cordialmente

Firma del padre o apoderado _____ Fecha _____

2 Actividad en familia

Práctica para la prueba estatal

Doblen la página a lo largo de las líneas punteadas. Resuelvan cada problema en otra hoja de papel. Luego, desdoblen la página y revisen las respuestas

1. Usen los datos de la siguiente tabla para calcular la media, la mediana, la moda y el rango etareo de los que trabajaron en el festival de primavera de la escuela intermedia Whetstone.

12	15	14	39	45	15
71	13	67	11	14	13
55	54	12	14	15	10
33	15	12	51	25	23

¿Qué selección incluye todas las respuestas correctas?

A media = 27; mediana = 15; modas = 12 y 14; rango = 81

B media = 28; mediana = 15; modas = 12 y 14; rango = 61

C media = 27; mediana = 15; moda = 15; rango = 61

D media = 27; mediana = 15; modas = 12 y 14; rango = 61

Doblen aquí.

- -

Solución

1. *Ayuda: Al calcular la media, la mediana, la moda y el rango siempre es mejor ordenar de menor a mayor un conjunto grande de números.*

   Para hallar la media, sumen todos los números y luego dividan entre la cantidad de números en el conjunto. Hay 24 números y la suma es 648. La media es 648 ÷ 24 ó 27. Esto elimina la opción B. No se necesita calcular la mediana ya que todas las opciones tienen el mismo valor. La moda es el número o números que aparecen más a menudo en el conjunto. Sólo la selección C tiene una media de 27 y una moda de 15.

   La respuesta es **C.**

2. Refiéranse a la tabla siguiente. ¿Durante qué mes los ciudadanos estadounidenses tenían menos probabilidad de estar desempleados?

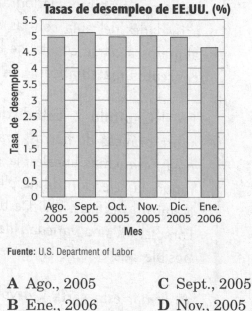

Tasas de desempleo de EE.UU. (%)

Fuente: U.S. Department of Labor

A Ago., 2005   **C** Sept., 2005
B Ene., 2006   **D** Nov., 2005

Solución

2. Los ciudadanos estadounidenses tienen menos posibilidad sufrir desempleo al estar más baja la tasa de empleo, lo cual corresponde a la barra más corta en la gráfica anterior. La barra más corta ocurre en enero, cuando el desempleo de los ciudadanos es menos probable.

   La respuesta es **B.**

2 Anticipation Guide

Statistics and Graphs

STEP 1 *Before you begin Chapter 2*

- Read each statement.

- Decide whether you Agree (A) or Disagree (D) with the statement.

- Write A or D in the first column OR if you are not sure whether you agree or disagree, write NS (Not Sure).

STEP 1 A, D, or NS	Statement	STEP 2 A or D
	1. A table can be used to help solve a problem when there is a multiple number of data in the problem.	
	2. A bar graph or a line graph can be used to display a set of data.	
	3. A stem-and-leaf plot is a graph that looks similar in shape to a tree.	
	4. The *mean* and the *average* of a set of numbers are the same.	
	5. The median of an ordered set of numbers is the middle number.	
	6. The range of a set of numbers is the sum of the numbers divided by the number of pieces of data.	
	7. Graphs are always accurate displays of data because they contain facts about the data.	
	8. Integers are the set of all positive whole numbers.	
	9. Positive integers are to the right of zero on a number line.	
	10. Opposite numbers are numbers that are the same distance from zero in opposite directions on the number line.	

STEP 2 *After you complete Chapter 2*

- Reread each statement and complete the last column by entering an A (Agree) or a D (Disagree).

- Did any of your opinions about the statements change from the first column?

- For those statements that you mark with a D, use a separate sheet of paper to explain why you disagree. Use examples, if possible.

Chapter Resources

2 Ejercicios preparatorios

Estadísticas y gráficas

PASO 1 *Antes de comenzar el Capítulo 2*

- Lee cada enunciado.

- Decide si estás de acuerdo (A) o en desacuerdo (D) con el enunciado.

- Escribe A o D en la primera columna O si no estás seguro(a) de la respuesta, escribe NS (No estoy seguro(a)).

PASO 1 A, D o NS	Enunciado	PASO 2 A o D
	1. Se puede usar una tabla como ayuda para resolver un problema cuando existe un número múltiple de datos en el problema.	
	2. Para exhibir un conjunto de datos se puede usar una gráfica de barras o una gráfica lineal.	
	3. Un diagrama de tallo y hojas es una gráfica que parece un árbol.	
	4. La media y el promedio de un conjunto de números son lo mismo.	
	5. La media en un conjunto ordenado de números es el número central.	
	6. El rango de un conjunto de números es la suma de los números dividida entre el número de datos.	
	7. Las gráficas son siempre exhibiciones precisas de datos porque contienen hechos acerca de los datos.	
	8. Los enteros son el conjunto de todos los números enteros positivos.	
	9. Los enteros positivos se ubican a la derecha de cero en una recta numérica.	
	10. Los números opuestos son números que están equidistantes de cero en direcciones opuestas en la recta numérica.	

PASO 2 *Después de completar el Capítulo 2*

- Vuelve a leer cada enunciado y completa la última columna con una A o una D.

- ¿Cambió cualquiera de tus opiniones sobre los enunciados de la primera columna?

- En una hoja de papel aparte, escribe un ejemplo de por qué estás en desacuerdo con los enunciados que marcaste con una D.

2-1 Study Guide and Intervention

Problem-Solving Investigation: Make a Table

When solving problems, one strategy that is helpful is to *make a table*. A table often makes it easy to clarify information in the problem. One type of table that is helpful to use is a *frequency table*, which shows the number of times each item or number appears.

You can use the *make a table* strategy, along with the following four-step problem-solving plan to solve a problem.

1 Understand – Read and get a general understanding of the problem.

2 Plan – Make a plan to solve the problem and estimate the solution.

3 Solve – Use your plan to solve the problem.

4 Check – Check the reasonableness of your solution.

Example 1

MOVIES Carlos took a survey of the students in his class to find out what type of movie they preferred. Using C for comedy, A for action, D for drama, and M for animated, the results are shown below. How many more students like comedies than action movies?

C A M M A C D C D C M A M M A C C D A C

Understand You need to find the number of students that chose comedies and the number of students that chose action. Then find the difference.

Plan Make a frequency table of the data.

Solve Draw and complete a frequency table.

7 people chose comedies and 5 people chose action. So, 7 − 5 or 2 more students chose comedy than action.

Check Go back to the list to verify there are 7 C's for comedy and 5 A's for action.

Favorite Type of Movie		
Movie Type	**Tally**	**Frequency**
comedy	⅞‖	7
action	⅞	5
drama	‖‖	3
animated	⅞	5

Exercise

GRADES The list below shows the quarterly grades for Mr. Vaquera's math class. Make a frequency table of the data. How many more students received a B than a D?

B C A A B D C B A C B B
B D A C B B C A A B A B

2-1 Skills Practice

Problem-Solving Investigation: Make a Table

Solve. Use the *make a table* strategy.

1. **BOOKS** Grace took a survey of the students in her class to find out their favorite types of books. Using S for science-fiction, A for adventure, B for biography, and R for romance, the results are shown below. Make a frequency table of the data. How many more students like science-fiction than adventure?

   S A S A A R S S S A R S B A B S S A R B

2. **SPORTS** The table below shows the position that students are trying out for on the school basketball team. Make a frequency table of the data. How many more students are trying out for forward than center?

Basketball Positions						
P	P	S	F	C	C	F
P	S	F	F	C	S	S
C	F	P	S	S	F	F

   P = point guard   S = shooting guard
   F = forward   C = center

3. **FRUIT JUICE** The table below shows the results of a survey of students' favorite fruit juice flavors. Make a frequency table of the data. How many more students like apple juice than pineapple juice?

Favorite Fruit Juice Flavors							
A	C	G	C	P	C	A	O
O	A	P	G	G	A	A	C
G	O	A	C	O	P	O	O

   A = apple   C = cranberry   G = grape
   O = orange   P = pineapple

2-1 Practice

Problem-Solving Investigation: Make a Table

Mixed Problem Solving

Use the make a table strategy to solve Exercise 1.

1. **BASKETBALL** The winning scores for teams in the National Wheelchair Basketball Association junior division for a recent season are shown. Make a frequency table of the data. How many winning scores were between 21 and 25?

NWBA Jr. Div. Winning Scores					
25	26	34	16	33	18
34	26	24	33	12	23

3. **SCIENCE** A biologist counted the birds she tagged and released each day for 20 days. Her counts were: 13, 14, 9, 16, 21, 8, 28, 25, 9, 13, 23, 16, 14, 9, 21, 25, 8, 10, 21, and 29. On how many days did she count between 6 and 10 birds or between 26 and 30 birds?

4. **TRAFFIC** The table shows the types of vehicles seen passing a street corner. Make a frequency table of the data. How many fewer motorcycles than cars were seen?

Types of Vehicles							
C	M	M	B	T	T	C	T
B	R	T	C	R	C	R	C
M	C	C	M	C	R	C	T

C = car   B = bicycle   T = truck
M = motorcycle   R = recreational vehicle

Use any strategy to solve Exercises 2–5. Some strategies are shown below.

Problem-Solving Strategies
• Guess and check.
• Make a table.

2. **MONEY** Emelio has 9 coins that total $2.21. He does not have a dollar coin. What are the coins?

5. **MONEY** Tonisha has $0 in her savings account. She deposits $40 every two weeks and withdraws $25 every four weeks. What will be her balance at the end of 24 weeks?

2-1 Word Problem Practice

Problem-Solving Investigation: Make a Table

1. **SPORTS** The table shows the result of Shante's survey of her classmates' favorite sports. How many more students chose softball/baseball than football?

Favorite Sports						
B	V	V	S	B	SB	SB
F	SB	B	S	V	F	B
B	SB	V	SB	SB	S	V

B = basketball   F = football   S = soccer
SB = softball/baseball   V = volleyball

2. **BASEBALL** The table shows the national league home run leaders in the 2002–2006 seasons. How many more home runs did Ryan Howard hit in 2006 than Jim Thome in 2003?

Year	Home Run Leader	Number of Home Runs
2002	Sammy Sosa	49
2003	Jim Thome	47
2004	Adrian Beltre	48
2005	Andruw Jones	51
2006	Ryan Howard	58

3. **MONEY** Trista has 8 coins in her pocket that total $1.55. She only has quarters and dimes. How many of each coin does Trista have?

4. **ORDER OF OPERATIONS** Use each of the symbols $+$, $-$, $\times$, and $\div$ to make the following math sentence true.

12 ____ 3 ____ 7 ____ 1 ____ 11 = 0

5. **GEOMETRY** Find the difference in the area of the rectangle and the area of the square.

3 m
9 m
5 m

6. **BICYCLES** Kenji is saving money to buy a new bicycle that costs $125. So far he has saved his weekly allowance of $5 for the past 8 weeks. He also saved $35 from his birthday money. How much more money does Kenji need to save?

2-2 **Lesson Reading Guide**

Bar Graphs and Line Graphs

Get Ready for the Lesson

**Complete the activity at the top of page 81 in your textbook.
Write your answers below.**

1. Which species has the most endangered animals?

2. Which species has the least endangered animals?

3. What might be an advantage of organizing data in a table?

4. Are there any disadvantages of organizing data in a table?

Read the Lesson

**Compare the frequency table at the top of page 81 with the bar graph
in the middle of the same page.**

5. How are they similar?

6. How are they different?

7. For purposes of comparison, which do you find easier to use to compare
   differences among frequencies—the frequency table or the bar graph?
   Explain.

Refer to the line graph at the bottom of page 82.

8. Use the same data to complete the table at
   the right.
9. Compare the table you just created with the
   line graph. Which do you think presents the
   data in a way that is easier to compare changes
   over periods of time? Explain.

Endangered U.S. Mammals	
Year	**Frequency**

Remember What You Learned

10. Explain how the information in a line graph differs from the information
    in a bar graph.

Lesson 2–2

2-2 Study Guide and Intervention

Bar Graphs and Line Graphs

A **graph** is a visual way to display data. A **bar graph** is used to compare data.
A **line graph** is used to show how data changes over a period of time.

Example 1 Make a bar graph of the data. Compare the number of students in jazz class with the number in ballet class.

Step 1 Decide on the scale and interval.

Step 2 Label the horizontal and vertical axes.

Step 3 Draw bars for each style.

Step 4 Label the graph with a title.

About twice as many students take ballet as take jazz.

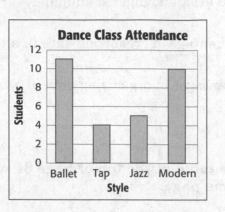

Dance Classes	
Style	Students
Ballet	11
Tap	4
Jazz	5
Modern	10

Example 2 Make a line graph of the data. Then describe the change in Gwen's allowance from 2003 to 2008.

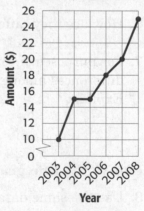

Gwen's Allowance						
Year	2003	2004	2005	2006	2007	2008
Amount ($)	10	15	15	18	20	25

Step 1 Decide on the scale and interval.

Step 2 Label the horizontal and vertical axes.

Step 3 Draw and connect the points for each year.

Step 4 Label the graph with a title.

Gwen's allowance did not change from 2004 to 2005 and then increased from 2005 to 2008.

Exercises

Make the graph listed for each set of data.

1. bar graph

Riding the Bus	
Student	Time (min)
Paulina	10
Omar	40
Ulari	20
Jacob	15
Amita	35

2. line graph

Getting Ready for School	
Day	Time (min)
Monday	34
Tuesday	30
Wednesday	37
Thursday	20
Friday	25

2-2 Skills Practice

Bar Graphs and Line Graphs

Make a bar graph for each set of data.

1.

Cars Made	
Country	**Cars (millions)**
Brazil	2
Japan	9
Germany	5
Spain	3
U.S.A.	6

2.

People in America in 1630	
Colony	**People (hundreds)**
Maine	4
New Hampshire	5
Massachusetts	9
New York	4
Virginia	25

Use the bar graph made in Exercise 1.

3. Which country made the greatest number of cars?

4. How does the number of cars made in Japan compare to the number made in Spain?

For Exercises 5 and 6, make a line graph for each set of data.

5.

Yuba County, California	
Year	**Population (thousands)**
1994	62
1996	61
1998	60
2000	60
2002	62
2004	65

6.

Everglades National Park	
Month	**Rainfall (inches)**
January	2
February	2
March	2
April	2
May	7
June	10

7. POPULATION Refer to the graph made in Exercise 5. Describe the change in Yuba County's population from 1994 to 2004.

8. WEATHER Refer to the graph made in Exercise 6. Describe the change in the amount of rainfall from January to June.

Lesson 2–2

2-2 Practice

Bar Graphs and Line Graphs

1. ANIMALS Make a bar graph of the data.

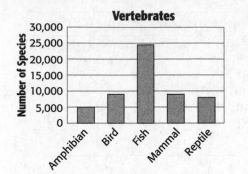

Vertebrates	
Class	Number of Species
Amphibians	5,000
Birds	9,000
Fish	24,500
Mammals	9,000
Reptiles	8,000

Source: *The World Almanac for Kids*

For Exercises 2 and 3, refer to the bar graph you made in Exercise 1.

2. Which animal classes have the same number of species?

3. Which animal class has about one third as many species as the fish class?

4. POPULATION Make a line graph of the data.

Population of the District of Columbia	
Year	Population (thousands)
1960	764
1970	757
1980	638
1990	607
2000	572

Source: U.S. Census Bureau

For Exercises 5 and 6, refer to the line graph you made in Exercise 4.

5. Describe the change in the District of Columbia population from 1970 to 2000.

6. What year showed the greatest change in population from the previous year?

BOOKS For Exercises 7 and 8, refer to the table.

7. Choose an appropriate scale and interval for the data set.

8. Would this data set be best represented by a bar graph or a line graph? Explain your reasoning.

Book Sales			
Week	Sales ($)	Week	Sales ($)
1	110	5	40
2	118	6	103
3	89	7	30
4	74	8	58

2-2 Word Problem Practice

Bar Graphs and Line Graphs

TREES For Exercises 1, 3, and 4, use Table A. For Exercises 2, 5, and 6, use Table B.

Table A

Average Heights of Pine Trees	
Tree	Height (ft)
Eastern White	75
Lodgepole	48
Longleaf	110
Pitch	55
Ponderosa	140

Table B

Lemons Produced by My Tree	
Year	Number of Lemons
2004	26
2005	124
2006	122
2007	78
2008	55

1. You and Jorge are writing a report on different kinds of pine trees. Make a bar graph for the report that shows the average heights of different kinds of pine trees. Use the data from Table A.

2. Table B shows the number of lemons your tree produced each year. Make a line graph for the data in Table B.

3. Use your graph for Exercise 1. Which tree is about half as tall as a ponderosa?

4. How does the average height of a pitch pine compare to the average height of a lodgepole pine?

5. Use the line graph you made in Exercise 2. Describe the change in fruit production for your lemon tree.

6. **FRUIT** Suppose you want to make a graph of the total number of lemons produced by your lemon tree and the total number of oranges produced by your orange tree in one year. Would you make a bar graph or a line graph? Explain.

Lesson 2-2

2-2 Enrichment

Line Plots

In a **line plot**, data are pictured on a number line. An ✕ is used to represent each item of data. For example, the figure below is a line plot that pictures data about the number of CDs owned by the students in a math class.

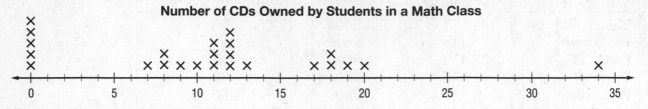

Number of CDs Owned by Students in a Math Class

Use the line plot above to answer each question.

1. How many students own exactly eighteen CDs?

2. What number of CDs is owned by exactly three students?

3. A data item that is far apart from the rest of the data is called an outlier. Is there an outlier among these data? What is it?

4. What would you say is the number of CDs owned by the "typical" student in this class?

5. Use the data in the table to complete the line plot below. Four data points have been graphed for you.

Number of Seconds for 24 Sixth Graders to Run 200 Meters											
130	100	85	120	100	100	110	150	90	100	110	130
125	105	100	70	125	85	95	130	105	90	105	100

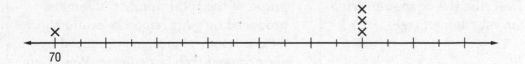

2-2 TI-83/84 Plus Activity

Line Graphs

You can view a variety of graphs on a graphing calculator. Follow the steps shown to display a line graph of the data in the table.

Average Cost of New Major League Baseball Team	
Team	Cost (millions)
1977	$7
1993	$95
1998	$130
2006	$450

Step 1 First, clear all lists. Then, enter the data from the first column of the table under L1.

Enter: `2nd` [MEM] 4 `ENTER` `STAT` `ENTER` 1977

`ENTER` 1993 `ENTER` 1998 `ENTER` 2006 `ENTER`

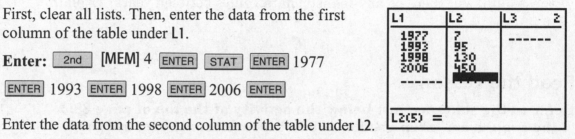

Step 2 Enter the data from the second column of the table under L2.

Enter: `▶` 7 `ENTER` 95 `ENTER` 130 `ENTER` 450 `ENTER`

Step 3 Define the graph.

Enter: `2nd` [STAT PLOT] `ENTER` `ENTER` `▼` `▶`

`ENTER` `▼` `2nd` [L1] `ENTER` `2nd` [L2]

`ENTER` `ZOOM` 9

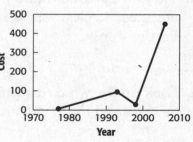

Display the data below in a line graph on a graphing calculator. (First, clear all lists.)

Number of Students Enrolled in 6th Grade	
Year	Students
2004	235
2005	219
2006	257
2007	289
2008	205

2-3 Lesson Reading Guide

Interpret Line Graphs

Get Ready for the Lesson

**Complete the activity at the top of page 88 in your textbook.
Write your answers below.**

1. Describe the trends in the winning amounts.

2. Predict how much the 2008 winner received. Research and compare to the actual 2008 amount.

3. The Masters Tournament is held once a year. If a line graph is made of these data, will there be any realistic data values between years? Explain.

Read the Lesson

**Refer to the sentence just below the activity at the top of page 88:
"Line graphs are often used to predict future events because they
show trends over time."**

3. The word *predict* comes from two Latin words that mean "to tell in advance." Look up the word *predict* in a dictionary. What meaning is given for the word?

4. Look up the word *trend* in a dictionary. What meaning is given for the word as it is used in the definition of line graph?

5. Look at the line graph at the bottom of page 88. In terms of trends, what happened between 2005 and 2008? What is the difference between prediction and data or statistics?

Remember What You Learned

6. Find two line graphs, one where you feel you can predict the future with confidence and one where you cannot. Explain the difference.

2-3 Study Guide and Intervention

Interpret Line Graphs

Because they show trends over time, **line graphs** are often used to predict future events.

Example 1 The graph shows the time Ruben spends each day practicing piano scales. Predict how much time he will spend practicing his scales on Friday.

Continue the graph with a dotted line in the same direction until you reach a vertical position for Friday. By extending the graph, you see that Ruben will probably spend half an hour practicing piano scales on Friday.

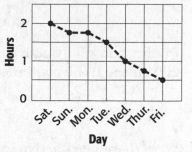

Piano Scale Practice Times

Exercises

MONEY Use the graph that shows the price of a ticket to a local high school football game over the last few years.

1. Has the price been increasing or decreasing? Explain.

2. Predict the price of a ticket in year 6 if the trend continues.

3. In what year do you think the price will reach $9.00 if the trend continues?

Football Tickets

BANKS Use the graph that shows the interest rate for a savings account over the last few years.

4. What does the graph tell you about interest rates?

5. If the trend continues, when will the interest rate reach 1 percent?

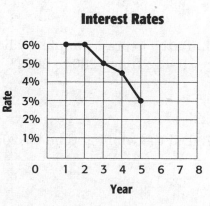

Interest Rates

Lesson 2-3

2-3 Skills Practice

Interpret Line Graphs

INTERNET Use the graph that shows Internet users in the United States.

1. Describe the change in active Internet users from February to March.

2. Predict how many active users there were in October 2004 if the trend continued.

3. Were there more active users in February 2004 or May 2004?

4. Based on your knowledge of Internet users, how do you anticipate the graph to change after September 2004?

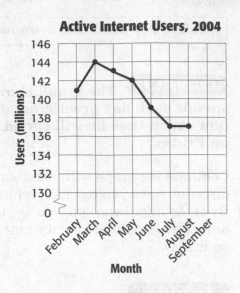

Active Internet Users, 2004

SPORTS Use the graph that shows the winning times of the 10K Biathlon rounded to the nearest minute.

5. How did the winning time change from 1980 to 2002?

6. To the nearest minute, by how much did the winning time change from 1980 to 2002?

7. Did the winning time for 2006 follow the trend?

8. Predict when the winning time will be less than 20 minutes if the trend continues.

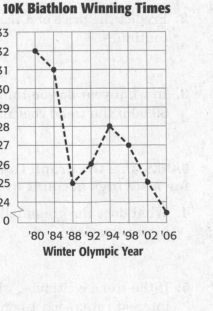

10K Biathlon Winning Times

2-3 Practice

Interpret Line Graphs

SPORTS For Exercises 1–3, use the graph at the right.

1. Describe the change in the number of swimsuits sold.

2. Predict the number of swimsuits sold in December. Explain your reasoning.

3. Predict the number of swimsuits sold in May. How did you reach this conclusion?

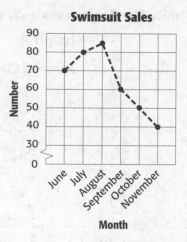

Swimsuit Sales

WEATHER For Exercises 4–7, use the graph at the right.

4. Predict the average temperature for Juneau in February.

5. Predict the average temperature for Mobile in October.

6. What do you think is the average temperature for San Francisco in October?

7. How much colder would you expect it to be in Juneau than in Mobile in October?

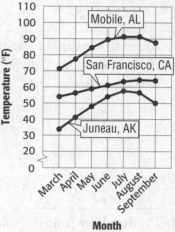

Average Monthly Temperature

Source: *The World Almanac*

BASEBALL For Exercises 8–10, use the table that shows the number of games won by the Florida Gators men's baseball team from 2002 to 2007.

Florida Gators Baseball Statistics						
Year	2002	2003	2004	2005	2006	2007
Games Won	46	37	43	48	28	29

8. Make a line graph of the data.

9. In what year did the team have the greatest increase in the number of games won?

10. Explain the disadvantages of using this line graph to make a prediction about the number of games that the team will win in 2009.

Lesson 2-3

2-3 **Word Problem Practice**

Interpret Line Graphs

FITNESS For Exercises 1–3, use Graph A. For Exercises 4–6, use Graph B.

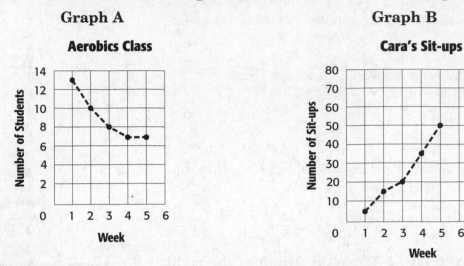

Graph A

Aerobics Class

Graph B

Cara's Sit-ups

1. Refer to Graph A. Describe the change in the number of students taking the aerobics class.	**2.** Predict how many students will be in the aerobics class in week 6 if the trend continues.
3. Predict how many students will be in the aerobics class in week 8.	**4.** Describe the change in the number of sit-ups Cara can do.
5. Predict how many sit-ups Cara will be able to do in week 6 if the trend continues.	**6.** Predict the week in which Cara will be able to do 80 sit-ups if the trend continues.

2-3 Enrichment

Graphs and Decision Making

Just as important as knowing how to make a graph, is deciding what type of graph to use. Here are some guidelines to help you make that decision.

• A **bar graph** compares data that fall into distinct categories, such as the populations of several cities compare in one year.

• A **line graph** shows changes in data over a period of time, such as the population of one city changing over several years.

• A **histogram** uses bars to represent the frequency of numerical data organized in intervals.

Would you use a bar graph, line graph, or histogram to show these data?

1. average temperatures in Sacramento for each month of the year

2. land area of continents

3. number of CD players purchased each year from 1999 through 2005

4. number of babies that weighed between 5 lb and 5 lb 15 oz, 6 lb and 6 lb 15 oz, 7 lb and 7 lb 15 oz, 8 lb and 8 lb 15 oz, or 9 lb and 9 lb 15 oz

Make an appropriate graph for each set of data.

5. Taxis in Use

Year	Number (millions)
2001	142
2002	148
2003	152
2004	154

6. Aircraft Capacity

Model	Number of Seats
B747	405
DC-10	288
L-1011	296
MD-80	142

7. Video Games Owned

Number of Games	Number of Students
0–2	5
3–5	4
6–8	9
9–11	6

Lesson 2-3

2-4 Lesson Reading Guide

Stem-and-Leaf Plots

Get Ready for the Lesson

Complete the activity at the top of page 92 in your textbook. Write your answers below.

1. What were the least and greatest number of instant messages sent?

2. Which number of instant messages occurred most often?

Read the Lesson

3. In a stem-and-leaf plot, in what order are the data?

4. In a stem-and-leaf plot of two-digit numbers, how are the data represented?

5. Look at the stem-and-leaf plot at the top of page 93. Of the twenty tallest waterfalls, how many are between 600 and 699 feet tall? Using the stem-and-leaf plot, how can you tell that this height-range is most common?

Remember What You Learned

6. Write the steps for making a stem-and-leaf plot. Show someone what a stem-and-leaf plot is, how to read one, and how to make one.

2-4 Study Guide and Intervention

Stem-and-Leaf Plots

Sometimes it is hard to read data in a table. You can use a **stem-and-leaf plot** to display the data in a more readable way. In a stem-and-leaf plot, you order the data from least to greatest. Then you organize the data by place value.

Example 1   Make a stem-and-leaf plot of the data in the table. Then write a few sentences that analyze the data.

Step 1 Order the data from least to greatest.
41 51 52 53 55 60 65 65 67 68 70 72

Step 2 Draw a vertical line and write the tens digits from least to greatest to the left of the line.

Step 3 Write the ones digits to the right of the line with the corresponding stems.

Money Earned Mowing Lawns ($)			
60	55	53	41
67	72	65	68
65	70	52	51

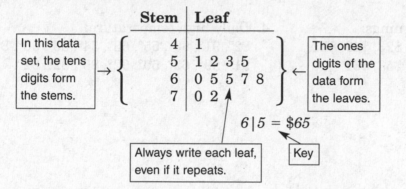

Stem	Leaf
4	1
5	1 2 3 5
6	0 5 5 7 8
7	0 2

In this data set, the tens digits form the stems.

The ones digits of the data form the leaves.

$6 \mid 5 = \$65$ Key

Always write each leaf, even if it repeats.

Step 4 Include a key that explains the stems and leaves.

By looking at the plot, it is easy to see that the least amount of money earned was $41 and the greatest amount was $72. You can also see that most of the data fall between $51 and $68.

Exercise

Make a stem-and-leaf plot for the set of data below. Write a few sentences that analyze the data.

Points scored: 34 44 51 48 55 41 47 22 55

Lesson 2-4

2-4   Skills Practice

Stem-and-Leaf Plots

Make a stem-and-leaf plot for each set of data.

1. Points scored in football games:
18, 16, 13, 20, 33, 58, 32, 14, 61, 67, 52

2. Quiz scores:
61, 75, 62, 63, 74, 71, 75, 82, 64, 81, 91, 65

3. Weekly baby-sitting earnings:
$52, $49, $37, $21, $65, $23, $49, $51,
$22, $21, $24, $47, $44, $53, $61

4. Daily high temperature:
82°, 91°, 80°, 55°, 63°, 54°, 83°, 90°, 84°,
91°, 59°, 62°, 50°, 92°, 85°, 92°, 92°

SPORTS For Exercises 5–8, use the stem-and-leaf plot that shows the total number of points earned by each volleyball team at a tournament.

Stem	Leaf
2	9
3	6 6 7 8 9
4	4 5 5 7 9
5	1 4 9
6	1 3 5

$4|5 = 45$ points

5. What was the greatest number of points earned?

6. What was the least number of points earned?

7. How many teams earned more than 50 points?

8. Between what numbers are most of the points earned?

2-4 Practice

Stem-and-Leaf Plots

Make a stem-and-leaf plot for each set of data.

1. Minutes on the bus to school:
   10, 5, 21, 30, 7, 12, 15, 21, 8, 12, 12, 20, 31, 10, 23, 31

2. Employee's ages:
   22, 52, 24, 19, 25, 36, 30, 32, 19, 26, 28, 33, 53, 24, 35, 26

SHOPPING For Exercises 3–5, use the stem-and-leaf plot at the right that shows costs for various pairs of jeans.

Stem	Leaf
1	6 6 7 8 8 9 9 9 9
2	1 3 5
3	
4	2 2 3

$2 \mid 3 = \$23$

3. How much is the most expensive pair of jeans?

4. How many pairs cost less than $20?

5. Write a sentence or two that analyzes the data.

6. Construct a stem-and-leaf plot for the set of test scores 81, 55, 55, 62, 73, 49, 56, 91, 55, 64, 72, 62, 64, 53, 56, and 57. Then write sentences explaining how a teacher might use the plot.

7. Display the amounts $104, $120, $99, $153, $122, $116, $114, $139, $102, $95, $123, $116, $152, $104 and $115 in a stem-and-leaf plot. (*Hint*: Use the hundreds and tens digits to form the stems.)

Lesson 2-4

2-4 Word Problem Practice

Stem-and-Leaf Plots

TRAFFIC For Exercises 1 and 2, use the table. For Exercises 3 and 4, use the stem-and-leaf plot.

Number of Trucks Passing Through the Intersection Each Hour					
5	15	6	42	34	28
19	18	19	22	23	21
32	26	34	19	29	21
10	6	8	40	14	17

Number of Birds at a Watering Hole Each Hour

Stem	Leaf
1	8 9
2	4 8 9
3	3 4 4 4
4	2 5 5 5 5 7 8
5	0 0 3 3 4 6 6 7

3|4 = 34 birds

1. Mr. Chin did a traffic survey. He wrote down the number of trucks that passed through an intersection each hour. Make a stem-and-leaf plot of his data.

2. Refer to your stem-and-leaf plot from Exercise 1. Mr. Chin needs to know the range of trucks passing through the intersection in one hour into which the greatest number of trucks fall.

3. What is the least number of birds at the watering hole in one hour? What is the greatest number?

4. What is the most frequent number of birds to be at the watering hole in one hour?

5. **RVs** Make a stem-and-leaf plot for the number of RVs Mr. Chin counted in 12 hours: 3, 4, 9, 13, 7, 9, 8, 5, 4, 6, 1, 11.

6. **RVs** Write a few sentences that analyze the RV data for Mr. Chin's report in Exercise 5.

30

2-4 Enrichment

A **back-to-back stem-and-leaf plot** is used to compare two sets of data. In this type of plot, the leaves for one set of data are on one side of the stems, and the leaves for the other set of data are on the other side of the stems. Two keys to the data are needed.

ELECTIONS Use the back-to-back stem-and-leaf plot of the electoral votes cast by each state and the District of Columbia for the Democratic and Republican candidates for U.S. president in 2004.

Democrat	Stem	Republican
3 3 3 4 4 4 4 7 7 9	0	3 3 3 3 3 4 5 5 5 5 5 6 6 6 7 7 8 8 9 9 9
0 0 1 2 5 7	1	0 1 1 1 3 5 5
1 1	2	0 7
1	3	4
	4	
5	5	

$3|0 = 3$ votes $0|3 = 3$ votes

1. What is the greatest number of electoral votes cast by a state for the Democratic candidate? the greatest number of electoral votes cast by a state for the Republican candidate?

2. Which candidate received votes from the greater number of states?

3. Which candidate received the greater number of total votes?

4. What is the difference between the number electoral votes cast for the candidates?

5. Write a sentence or two comparing the number of electoral votes cast for the two candidates.

Lesson 2-4

2-5 Lesson Reading Guide

Line Plots

Get Ready for the Lesson

Read the introduction at the top of page 96 in your textbook. Write your answers below.

1. How many of the animals have a life expectancy of 15 years?

2. How many animals have a life expectancy from 5 to 10 years, including 10?

3. What is the longest life expectancy represented?

4. What is the shortest life expectancy represented?

Read the Lesson

5. How is a line plot similar to plotting points on a number line?

6. Describe one benefit of plotting data on a line plot.

7. Explain how you can use a line plot to find out how spread out a group of data are.

Remember What You Learned

8. Work with a partner. Find a set of data from a survey, newspaper, or the Internet that can be used in a line plot. Create a line plot of the data along with two questions about the data. Switch your line plot and questions with another group. Use the line plots to answer the questions about the data.

2-5 Study Guide and Intervention

Line Plots

A **line plot** is a diagram that shows the frequency of data on a number line. A line plot is created by drawing a number line and then placing an × above a data value each time that data occurs.

Example 1 Make a line plot of the data in the table at the right.

Time Spent Traveling to School (minutes)						
5	6	3	10	12	15	5
10	5	8	12	5	5	8

Draw a number line. The smallest value is 3 minutes and the largest value is 15 minutes. So, you can use a scale of 0 to 15.

Put an × above the number that represents the travel time of each student in the table. Be sure to include a title.

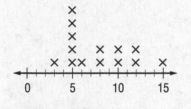

Example 2 How many students spend 5 minutes traveling to school each day?

Locate 5 on the number line and count the number of ×'s above it. There are 5 students that travel 5 minutes to school each day.

Exercises

AGES For Exercises 1–3, use the data below.

Ages of Lifeguards at Brookville Swim Club					
16	18	16	20	22	18
18	17	18	25	17	19

1. Make a line plot of the data.

2. How many of the lifeguards are 18 years old?

3. What is the age difference between the oldest and youngest lifeguard at Brookville Swim Club?

Lesson 2–5

2-5 Skills Practice

Line Plots

Make a line plot for each set of data.

1.

Average Points Per Game for NBA Leading Scorers				
25	25	30	30	21
21	22	26	25	21

2.

Daily High Temperature for a 2-Week Period (°F)						
71	71	75	65	65	68	71
62	70	71	65	70	72	72

GRADES For Exercises 3–6, use the line plot below.

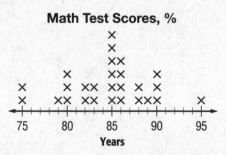

Math Test Scores, %

3. How many students had a score of 80% on the math test?

4. Which test score did the most students score on the math test?

5. What is the difference between the highest and lowest test score?

6. Write one or two sentences that analyze the data.

2-5 Practice

Line Plots

PRESIDENTS For Exercises 1–4, use the line plot below. It shows the ages of the first ten Presidents of the United States when they first took office.

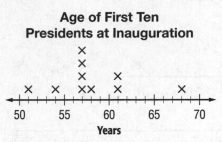

Age of First Ten Presidents at Inauguration

Source: *Time Almanac*

1. How many Presidents were 54 when they took office?

2. Which age was most common among the first ten Presidents when they took office?

3. How many Presidents were in their 60s when they first took office?

4. What is the difference between the age of the oldest and youngest President represented in the line plot?

5. **EXERCISE** Make a line plot for the set of data.

Miles Walked this Week			
16	21	11	24
8	14	16	11
21	10	8	14
11	24	12	18
18	27	11	14

BIRDS For Exercises 6 and 7, use the line plot below. It shows the number of mockingbirds each bird watcher saw on a bird walk.

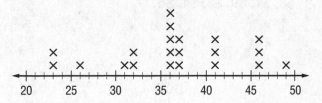

6. How many more bird watchers saw 36 mockingbirds than saw 46 mockingbirds?

7. How many bird watchers are represented in the line plot?

Lesson 2–5

2-5 Word Problem Practice

Line Plots

ANIMALS For Exercises 1–4, use the line plot below about the maximum speed of several animals.

Maximum Speed of Animals (miles per hour)

1. How many animals represented in the line plot have a maximum speed of 45 miles per hour?

2. What speed is most common that is represented in the line plot?

3. What is the difference between the greatest speed and least speed represented in the line plot?

4. Write one or two sentences that analyze the data.

5. **LAWN SERVICE** Make a line plot for the amount of money Kyle earned this summer with each lawn service job: $20, $25, $30, $15, $22, $25, $25, $30, $18, $15, $25, $20.

6. **MAGAZINES** Make a line plot for the selling price of several popular magazines: $3, $4, $5, $4, $3, $2, $4, $5, $3, $7, $9, $3, $4, $5.

2-5 Enrichment

Line Plots and Bar Graphs

A line plot is a version of a bar graph. Look at the line plot on the right. It shows the results of a survey about TV viewing habits. Twenty-two students were asked how many hours of television they watch in one week. Three students said they watch 2 hours of television each week. Two students said they watch 9 hours of television per week.

A bar graph is another way to display data. You can use a line plot to create a bar graph. First, draw a vertical line up from zero to form the *y*-axis. Decide on an interval for the *y*-axis. Draw horizontal lines across from the numbers. Draw bars over the *x*'s and shade them in. Label the *y*-axis "Number of Students" and the *x*-axis "Number of Hours."

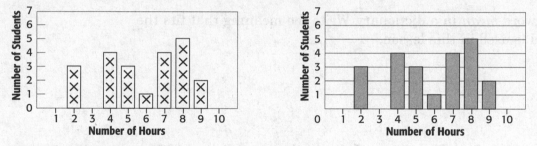

Change each line plot into a bar graph.

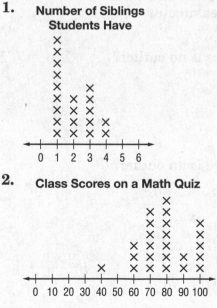

1. **Number of Siblings Students Have**

2. **Class Scores on a Math Quiz**

3. **Number of Hours Playing Sports per Week**

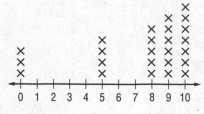

Lesson 2-5

2-6 Lesson Reading Guide

Mean

Get Ready for the Lesson

Complete the Mini Lab at the top of page 102 in your textbook. Write your answers below.

1. On average, how many inches did it snow per day in five days? Explain your reasoning.

2. Suppose on the sixth day it snowed 9 inches. If you moved the cubes again, how many cubes would be in each stack?

Read the Lesson

3. Look up the word *mean* in a dictionary. Write the meaning that fits the way the word is used in this lesson.

Look at the paragraph below the activity at the top of page 102 in your textbook. A number that helps describe all of the data in a data set is an average. An average is also referred to as a measure of central tendency.

4. Is the mean a good measure of central tendency when there is no outlier? Give an example.

5. Is the mean a good measure of central tendency when there is an outlier? Give an example.

Remember What You Learned

6. Explain one problem with using the mean as a measure of central tendency.

2-6 Study Guide and Intervention

Mean

> The **mean** is the most common measure of central tendency. It is an average, so it describes all of the data in a data set.

Example 1 The picture graph shows the number of members on four different swim teams. Find the mean number of members for the four different swim teams.

Simplify an expression.

$$\text{mean} = \frac{9 + 11 + 6 + 10}{4}$$

$$= \frac{36}{4} \text{ or } 9$$

Swim Team Members	
Amberly	𝕏𝕏𝕏𝕏𝕏𝕏𝕏𝕏𝕏
Carlton	𝕏𝕏𝕏𝕏𝕏𝕏𝕏𝕏𝕏𝕏𝕏
Hamilton	𝕏𝕏𝕏𝕏𝕏𝕏
Westhigh	𝕏𝕏𝕏𝕏𝕏𝕏𝕏𝕏𝕏𝕏

> A set of data may contain very high or very low values. These values are called **outliers**.

Example 2 Find the mean for the snowfall data with and without the outlier. Then tell how the outlier affects the mean of the data.

Compared to the other values, 4 inches is low. So, it is an outlier.

Month	Snowfall (in.)
Nov.	20
Dec.	19
Jan.	20
Feb.	17
Mar.	4

mean with outlier

$$\text{mean} = \frac{20 + 19 + 20 + 17 + 4}{5}$$

$$= \frac{80}{5} \text{ or } 16$$

mean without outlier

$$\text{mean} = \frac{20 + 19 + 20 + 17}{4}$$

$$= \frac{76}{4} \text{ or } 19$$

With the outlier, the mean is less than the values of most of the data. Without the outlier, the mean is close in value to the data.

Exercises

SHOPPING For Exercises 1–3, use the bar graph at the right.

1. Find the mean of the data.

2. Which jacket price is an outlier?

3. Find the mean of the data if the outlier is not included.

4. How does the outlier affect the mean of the data?

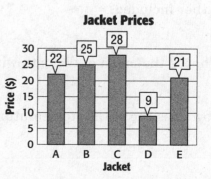

Jacket Prices

2-6 Skills Practice

Mean

Find the mean of the data represented in each model.

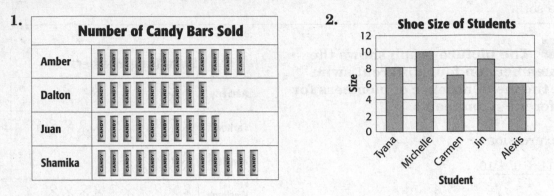

1.

Number of Candy Bars Sold

Amber	CANDY CANDY CANDY CANDY CANDY CANDY CANDY CANDY CANDY CANDY CANDY
Dalton	CANDY CANDY CANDY CANDY CANDY CANDY CANDY
Juan	CANDY CANDY CANDY CANDY CANDY CANDY CANDY CANDY CANDY
Shamika	CANDY CANDY CANDY CANDY CANDY CANDY CANDY CANDY CANDY CANDY

2.

Shoe Size of Students

Identify the outlier or outliers in each set of data.

3.

Price	Tally	Frequency
$10	IIII	4
$20	HH	5
$30	III	3
$40	I	1

4.

Stem	Leaf
2	0 1 4 7
3	0 0 1 5 6
4	3 6
5	7

$$2 \mid 4 = 24$$

WEATHER Use the data in the table that shows daily temperatures.

Day	Temp. (°F)
Monday	69
Tuesday	70
Wednesday	73
Thursday	35
Friday	68

5. Identify the outlier.

6. What is the mean of the data with the outlier included?

7. What is the mean of the data without the outlier included?

8. How does the outlier temperature affect the mean of the data?

2-6 Practice

Mean

Find the mean of the data represented in each model.

1.

Number of Toys Collected	
Ling	🧸🧸🧸🧸🧸🧸
Kathy	🧸🧸🧸🧸🧸🧸🧸🧸🧸
Lucita	🧸🧸🧸🧸🧸🧸🧸🧸🧸🧸
Terrell	🧸🧸🧸🧸🧸

2.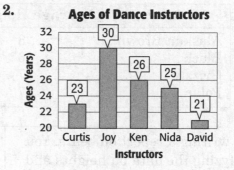

NATURE For Exercises 3–6, use the table that shows the heights of the tallest waterfalls along Oregon's Columbia River Gorge.

3. Find the mean of the data.

4. Identify the outlier.

5. Find the mean if Multnomah Falls is not included in the data set.

6. How does the outlier affect the mean of the data?

Falls	Height (ft)
Bridal Veil	153
Horsetail	176
Latourell	249
Metlako	150
Multnomah	620
Wahkeena	242

Source: U.S. Forest Service

GARDENING For Exercises 7–9, use the following information.

Alan earned $23, $26, $25, $24, $23, $24, $6, $24, and $23 gardening.

7. What is the mean of the amounts he earned?

8. Which amount is an outlier?

9. How does the outlier affect the mean of the data?

Find the mean for number of cans collected. Explain the method you used.

10. 57, 59, 60, 58, 58, 56

2-6 Word Problem Practice

Mean

ANIMALS For Exercises 1–3, use the table about bears.

Bear	Average Height (ft)	Average Weight (lb)
Alaskan Brown	8	1,500
Black	6	338
Grizzly	7	588
Polar	7	850

1. You are writing a report on bears. You are analyzing the data on heights and weights in the table above. First look for outliers. Identify the outlier for the height data. Identify the outlier for the weight data.

2. Find the mean of the bear weight data with and without the outlier.

3. Describe how the outlier affects the mean of the bear weight data.

4. WORK Carlos earned $23, $29, $25, $16, and $17 working at an ice cream shop after school. What is the mean amount he earned?

5. CARS The cost of a tank of gas at nine different gas stations is shown below. What was the mean cost of a tank of gas?

Cost of Gas: $17, $18, $22, $15, $17, $16, $25, $21, and $20

6. SCHOOL Sally received scores on math quizzes as shown below. Find her mean score with and without both outliers.

Quiz Scores: 84, 85, 91, 81, 52, 92, 99, 91, and 45

2-6 Enrichment

Mean, Median, or Mode?

When most people hear the word "average," they think about what mathematicians call arithmetic mean. But the three measures of central tendency, mean, median and mode, are all different types of averages. Average is not a mathematical word. In mathematics, it is necessary to specify which type of average you are using.

1. The prices of seven homes for sale in Sunnydale are $151,000; $148,500; $163,000; $180,500; $151,000; $172,000; $189,000. Find the mean, median, and mode for the price of the homes for sale.

2. A real estate agent is writing an advertisement for a newspaper. She writes, "The average price of a home in Sunnydale is $151,000." Which average did she use? Explain why she chose to use this particular average. Is this average misleading?

3. Which type of average should be used to best represent the "average" price of a home in Sunnydale?

A candy company is having a special promotion for which it includes special blue colored candies in its packages. The line plot shows how many blue candies were found in each of 19 packages.

```
                              ×
     ×             ×   ×
     ×     ×       ×   ×
     ×     ×   ×   ×   ×
     ×     ×   ×   ×   ×   ×
   +---+---+---+---+---+---+---+---+
     0   1   2   3   4   5   6   7
```

Sam, Matt, and Carla solve to find the average number of blue candies per package. None of the students finds the same answer. Sam has the highest value, then Carla, and Matt's answer is has the lowest value. Their teacher tells them that each one has a correct answer.

4. Determine which average each student found.

5. Find the mean, median, and mode for the line plot.

6. Matt looks at the line plot and notices that the number he found as average was never plotted. Matt decides that since that number of candies was never found in the bags, it can't be the average. Explain why the number is still considered an average.

2-6 Scientific Calculator Activity

Finding the Mean

A calculator can be used to find the mean (average) of a set of data.

Example Erick bought 5 compact discs. If he paid $12, $15, $18, $11, and $10, what was the mean price he paid for a compact disc?

Enter: (12 [+] 15 [+] 18 [+] 11

[+] 10) [÷] 5 [ENTER =] 13.2

The average price of a disc was $13.20.

Find the mean for each set of data.

1.

Test Scores
98
84
91
79
88

Mean Score:

2.

Bank Deposits
$128
$352
$421
$51
$532
$87
$137

Mean Deposit:

3.

Daily Temperatures (°Fahrenheit)	
High	Low
87°	68°
79°	54°
87°	60°
91°	74°
67°	64°
72°	49°

Mean High Temp.:

Mean Low Temp.:

Overall Mean Temp.:

4.

20-Point Quiz Scores			
19	18	16	20
17	15	12	19
20	12	11	9
16	19	17	14
10	16	15	13
15	11	9	12
15	10	7	19

Mean Score:

2-6 TI-73 Activity

Finding the Mean

Use the TI-73 calculator to find the mean (average) of a set of data.

Example Erick bought 5 compact discs. He paid $12, $15, $18, $11, and $10. What is the mean price he paid for a compact disc?

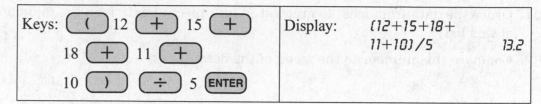

| Keys: (12 + 15 + 18 + 11 + 10) ÷ 5 ENTER | Display: (12+15+18+ 11+10)/5   13.2 |

The average price of a disc was $13.20.

You can also use the List feature to calculate the mean.

Step 1 Clear all lists.
Keys: 2nd [MEM] 6 ENTER

Step 2 Select List. LIST

Step 3 Enter each value in L1, and press ENTER after each one.
Return to Home screen.
2nd [QUIT]

Step 4 Select Mean and L1.
2nd [STAT] ▶ ▶ 3 2nd [STAT] ENTER ENTER

Find the mean for each set of data.

1.

Test Scores				
98	84	91	79	88

Mean Score:

2.

Bank Deposits						
$128	$352	$421	$51	$532	$87	$137

Mean Deposit:

3.

Daily Temperatures (°Fahrenheit)						
High	87°	79°	87°	91°	67°	72°
Low	68°	54°	60°	74°	64°	49°

Mean High Temp.:
Mean Low Temp.:
Overall Mean Temp.:

4.

20-Point Quiz Scores						
19	17	20	16	10	15	15
18	15	12	19	16	11	10
16	12	11	17	15	9	7
20	19	9	14	13	12	19

Mean Score:

Lesson 2-6

2-7 Lesson Reading Guide
Median, Mode, and Range

Get Ready for the Lesson

**Complete the activity at the top of page 108 in your textbook.
Write your answers below.**

1. Order the data from least to greatest. Which piece of data is in the middle of this list?

2. Compare this number to the mean of the data.

Read the Lesson

3. How are mean, median, and mode similar? How are they different?

Look at Example 4 on page 110.

4. How would you find the average of the data? What is another term for the average of the data?

5. What is causing the mean to be so high?

6. If there were two deserts of 250,000 square miles, how would this affect the mean?

7. Does this example illustrate the statement, "Some averages may describe a data set better than other averages"?

Remember What You Learned

8. You may already know that a median strip refers to the concrete or landscaped divider that runs down the center of many roads. How does this idea of median relate to the meaning of median in this lesson?

2-7 Study Guide and Intervention

Median, Mode, and Range

> The **median** is the middle number of the data put in order, or the mean of the middle two numbers.
> The **mode** is the number or numbers that occur most often.

Example 1 The table shows the costs of seven different books. Find the mean, median, and mode of the data.

Book Costs ($)			
22	13	11	16
14	13	16	

mean: $\dfrac{22 + 13 + 11 + 16 + 14 + 13 + 16}{7} = \dfrac{105}{7}$ or 15

To find the median, write the data in order from least to greatest.
median: 11, 13, 13, ⑭ 16, 16, 22

To find the mode, find the number or numbers that occur most often.
mode: 11, ⑬ ⑬ 14, ⑯ ⑯ 22

The mean is $15. The median is $14. There are two modes, $13 and $16.

> Whereas the measures of central tendency describe the average of a set of data, the **range** of a set of data describes how the data vary.

Example 2 Find the range of the data in the stem-and-leaf plot. Then write a sentence describing how the data vary.

Stem	Leaf
3	2
4	0
5	0 5
6	0 3

$3 \mid 2 = 32°$

The greatest value is 63. The least value is 32. So, the range is 63° − 32° or 31°. The range is large. It tells us that the data vary greatly in value.

Exercises

Find the mean, median, mode, and range of each set of data.

1. hours worked: 14, 13, 14, 16, 8

2. points scored by football team: 29, 31, 14, 21, 31, 22, 20

3.

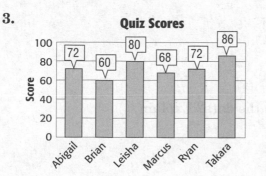

Quiz Scores

4.

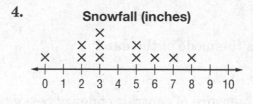

Snowfall (inches)

2-7 Skills Practice

Median, Mode, and Range

Find the median, mode, and range for each set of data.

1. age of children Danielle babysits:
   6, 9, 2, 4, 3, 6, 5

2. hours spent studying:
   13, 6, 7, 13, 6

3. age of grandchildren:
   1, 15, 9, 12, 18, 9, 5, 14, 7

4. points scored in video game:
   13, 7, 17, 19, 7, 15, 11, 7

5. amount of weekly allowances:
   3, 9, 4, 3, 9, 4, 2, 3, 8

6. height of trees in feet:
   25, 18, 14, 27, 25, 14, 18, 25, 23

Find the mean, median, mode, and range of the data represented.

7. Annual Rainfall

Stem	Leaf
2	1 3 7 8
3	2 2 4
4	3

   3 | 2 = 32 in.

8.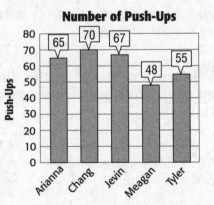

MUSEUMS Use the table showing the number of visitors to the art museum each month.

Vistors to the Art Museum (thousands)			
3	11	5	4
5	3	6	3
12	2	2	4

9. What is the mean of the data?

10. What is the median of the data?

11. What is the mode of the data?

12. Which measure of central tendency best describes the data? Explain.

2-7 Practice

Median, Mode, and Range

Find the median, mode, and range for each set of data.

1. minutes spent practicing violin:
25, 15, 30, 25, 20, 15, 24

2. snow in inches:
40, 28, 24, 37, 43, 26, 30, 36

Find the mean, median, mode, and range of the data represented in each statistical graph.

3.

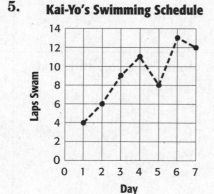

4.

Stem	Leaf
4	1 2 4 4
5	2 4
6	1 3 4 7 7 7 7 8 8
7	2 2 3
8	0 1 2 4 5 6

5|4 = $54

5. **Kai-Yo's Swimming Schedule**

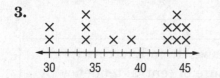

6. **Student's Favorite Music**

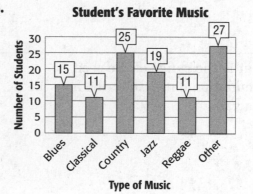

WEATHER For Exercises 7–9, refer to the table at the right.

7. Compare the median low temperatures.

8. Find the range for each data set.

9. Write a statement that compares the daily low temperatures for the two cities.

Daily Low Temperatures (°F)	
Charleston	**Atlanta**
33 34 33 35	48 41 43 40
36 35 34	45 35 37

Lesson 2-7

2-7 Word Problem Practice

Median, Mode, and Range

SCIENCE For Exercises 1–3, use Table A. For Exercises 4–6, use Table B. Table A shows the number of days it took for some seeds to germinate after planting. Table B shows how tall the plants were after 60 days.

Table A

Number of Days for Seeds to Germinate				
15	20	30	15	16
9	21	21	15	

Table B

Height (in.) of Plants After 60 Days				
17	19	13	17	20
15	17	21	14	

1. Refer to Table A. You are doing some experiments with germinating seeds. You are preparing a report on your findings to a seed company. What are the mean, median, and mode of the data?

2. Use your answer from Exercise 1. Which measure of central tendency best describes the data? Explain.

3. What is the range of the seed germination data? Describe how the data vary.

4. What are the mean, median, and mode of the plant height data?

5. Refer to your answer in Exercise 4. Which measure of central tendency best describes the data? Explain.

6. What is the range of the plant height data? Describe how the data vary.

2-7 **Enrichment**

Puzzling Over Data

Each puzzle on this page contains an incomplete set of data. The clues give you information about the mean, median, mode, or range of the data. Working from these clues, you can decide what the missing data items must be. For example, this is how you might solve the data puzzle at the right.

Clue: mean = 18

Data: 12, 17, 18, 19, 19, ☐

There are 6 items of data.
The mean is 18, so the sum of the data must be $6 \times 18 = 108$.
Add the given data: $12 + 17 + 18 + 19 + 19 = 85$.
Subtract from 108: $108 - 85 = 23$.

So the complete set of data is: 12, 17, 18, 19, 19, 23 .

Find the missing data. (Assume that the data items are listed in order from least to greatest.)

1. *Clue*:   mode = 8

   Data: 7, 7, 8, ☐, ☐, 14

2. *Clue*:   median = 54.5

   Data: 36, 40, 49, ☐, 65, 84

3. *Clues*:   mean = 27
   mode = 30

   Data: 10, 25, 27, ☐, 30, ☐

4. *Clues*:   median = 120
   range = 46

   Data: 110, 112, ☐, 124, 136, ☐

5. *Clues*:   mean = 13
   median = 13
   range = 13

   Data: ☐, 9, 12, ☐, 18, ☐

6. *Clues*:   mean = 7
   median = 8.5
   mode = 10

   Data: ☐, 4, 8, ☐, ☐, ☐

7. *Clues*:   mean = 60
   mode = 52
   range = 28

   Data: ☐, 52, ☐, ☐, 72, 78

8. *Clues*:   median = 24
   mode = 28
   range = 24

   Data: 6, 15, ☐, ☐, ☐, ☐

Lesson 2-7

2-7 Spreadsheet Activity

Median, Mode, and Range

A spreadsheet is an excellent tool for working with and analyzing numerical data. You can use a spreadsheet to find the median, mode, and range for a set of data.

Example Use a spreadsheet to find the median, mode, and range for the set {15, 15, 16, 17, 18, 19, 12, 11, 15, 18, 19, 20}.

Use the second column of the spreadsheet to enter the data. Enter the numbers using the formula bar. Click on a cell of the spreadsheet, type the number and press ENTER.

Find the median of the data in the cell below the last of the data. To do this, enter =MEDIAN(B1:B12). Notice that the data is in cells B1 to B12. Then press ENTER. This returns the median value of 16.5.

Find the mode of the data in the cell below the range. Enter =MODE(B1:B12). Then press ENTER. This returns the mode of 15.

Find the range of the data in the cell below the mode by subtracting the minimum value from the maximum value. Enter =MAX(B1:B12)−MIN(B1:B12). Press ENTER. The range is 9.

	A	B	C
1		15	
2		15	
3		16	
4		17	
5		18	
6		19	
7		12	
8		11	
9		15	
10		18	
11		19	
12		20	
13	median	16.5	
14	mode	15	
15	range	9	
16			

Sheet 1

Use a spreadsheet to find the median, mode, and range for each set of data.

1. {25, 32, 31, 32, 30, 19, 40}

2. {9, 9, 10, 7, 8, 5, 4, 6, 9}

3. {90, 70, 85, 65, 71, 85}

4. {14, 16, 7, 2, 3, 6, 21, 21}

5. {2.2, 2.5, 2.3, 2.5, 2.1, 2.8}

6. {5, 5, 5, 6, 6, 7, 4, 3, 1, 0}

7. {112, 118, 147, 123, 194}

8. {0.4, 0.9, 0.1, 0.6, 0.6, 0.8}

2-8 Lesson Reading Guide

Selecting an Appropriate Display

Get Ready for the Lesson

Read the introduction at the top of page 114 in your textbook. Write your answers below.

1. Which display allows you to find a rabbit's maximum speed?

2. In which display is it easier to find the range of the data?

Read the Lesson

3. Write an example of data that is best displayed in a bar graph.

4. Write an example of data that is best displayed in a line graph.

5. Write an example of data that is best displayed in a line plot.

6. Write an example of data that is best displayed in a stem-and-leaf plot.

Remember What You Learned

7. Use a magazine, newspaper, or the Internet to find data that is represented in a bar graph, line graph, line plot, or stem-and-leaf plot. Examine the data to see if it is represented in the most appropriate display. Are there other displays in which the data could be represented?

Lesson 2-8

2-8 Study Guide and Intervention

Selecting an Appropriate Display

Data can be displayed in many different ways, including the following:

- A **bar graph** shows the number of items in a specific category.
- A **line graph** shows change over a period of time.
- A **line plot** shows how many times each number occurs in the data.
- A **stem-and-leaf plot** lists all individual numerical data in a condensed form.

Example 1 Which display allows you to see how art show ticket prices have changed since 2004.

Art Show Ticket Prices

Art Show Ticket Prices

The line graph allows you to see how the art show ticket prices have increased since 2004.

Example 2 What type of display would you use to show the results of a survey of students' favorite brand of tennis shoes.

Since the data would list the number of students that chose each brand, or category, the data would best be displayed in a bar graph.

Exercises

1. **GRADES** Which display makes it easier to see how many students had test scores in the 80s?

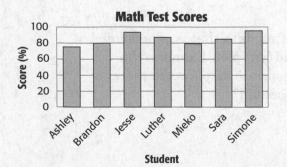

Math Test Scores

Stem	Leaf
7	5 9
8	0 5 8
9	2 3

$8|0 = 80\%$

2. **VOLLEYBALL** What type of display would you use to show the number of wins the school volleyball team had from 2000 to 2005?

2-8 ## Skills Practice

Selecting an Appropriate Display

1. **ANIMALS** Which display makes it easier to compare the average weight of a bulldog with the average weight of a pug?

Average Weight of Dogs

Stem	Leaf
0	4 6
1	6
2	6
3	
4	
5	0
6	0
7	0

$0|4 = 4\ lb$

Average Weight of Dogs

Average Weight (pounds)

Beagle 26, Boxer 70, Bulldog 50, Chihuahua 4, Dalmation 60, Pug 16, Yorkshire 6

Breed

Select an appropriate type of display for data gathered about each situation.

2. the record high temperature for each month this year

3. the test scores each student had on a science test

4. the favorite topping on a pizza of the students in Mrs. Witsken's class

5. Edmund's weight on his birthday over the past 10 years

6. Select and make an appropriate type of display.

Company Sales	
Year	**Sales ($ millions)**
2004	4.0
2005	4.5
2006	4.0
2007	5.5
2008	6.0
2009	8.0

Lesson 2-8

2-8 Practice

Selecting an Appropriate Display

1. **FOOD** Which display makes it easier to see the median cost of providing food stamps from 1998 to 2003?

Stem	Leaf
1	7 8 8 9
2	1 4

$1|7 = 17$ thousand million dollars

Source: *The World Almanac*

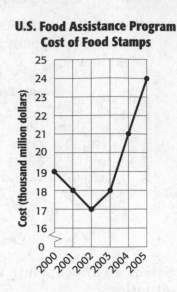

U.S. Food Assistance Program
Cost of Food Stamps

Select an appropriate type of display for data gathered about each situation. Sample answers are given.

2. the heights of buildings in town
3. the number of cars a dealer sold each month over the past year
4. the number of scores made by each team member in a basketball season
5. **OLYMPICS** Select an appropriate type of display for the data. Then make a display.

Olympic Hammer Throw Winners			
Year	Distance (m)	Year	Distance (m)
1968	73	1988	85
1972	76	1992	83
1976	78	1996	81
1980	82	2000	80
1984	78	2004	83

6. **GEOGRAPHY** Display the data in the bar graph using another type of display. Compare the displays.

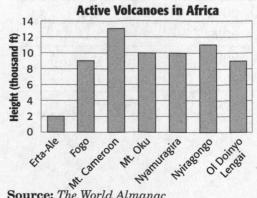

Active Volcanoes in Africa

Source: *The World Almanac*

2-8 **Word Problem Practice**

Selecting an Appropriate Display

VIDEOS For Exercises 1–4, use the three graphs on DVD sales shown below.

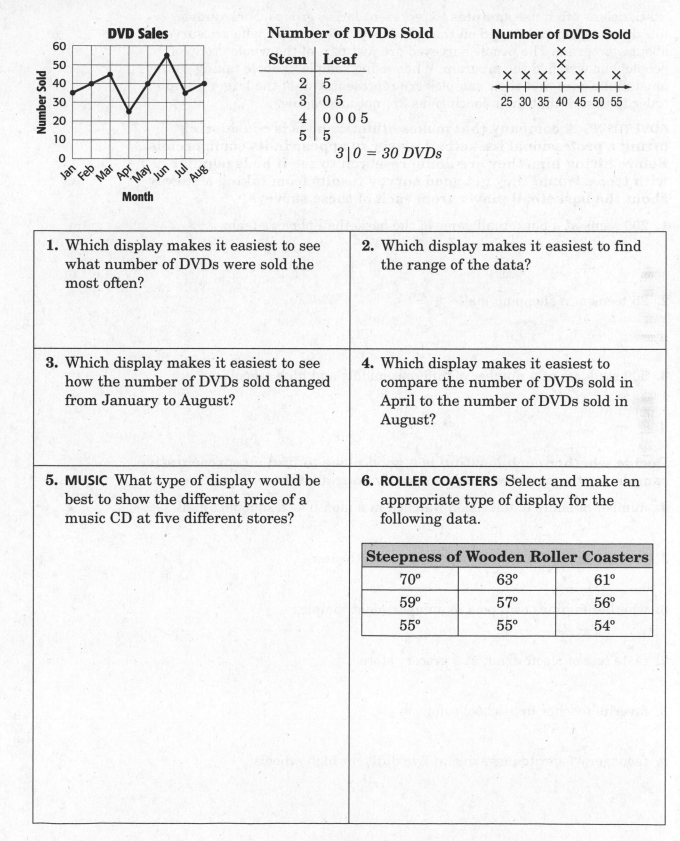

DVD Sales

Number of DVDs Sold

Stem	Leaf
2	5
3	0 5
4	0 0 0 5
5	5

$3|0 = 30$ DVDs

Number of DVDs Sold

1. Which display makes it easiest to see what number of DVDs were sold the most often?

2. Which display makes it easiest to find the range of the data?

3. Which display makes it easiest to see how the number of DVDs sold changed from January to August?

4. Which display makes it easiest to compare the number of DVDs sold in April to the number of DVDs sold in August?

5. **MUSIC** What type of display would be best to show the different price of a music CD at five different stores?

6. **ROLLER COASTERS** Select and make an appropriate type of display for the following data.

Steepness of Wooden Roller Coasters		
70°	63°	61°
59°	57°	56°
55°	55°	54°

2-8 Enrichment

Choosing a Representative Sample

Statisticians often use **samples** to represent larger groups. For example, television ratings are based on the opinions of a few people who are surveyed about a program. The people surveyed are just part of the whole group of people who watched the program. When using samples, people taking surveys must make sure that their samples are representative of the larger group in order to ensure that their conclusions are not misleading.

ADVERTISING A company that makes athletic shoes is considering hiring a professional basketball player to appear in its commercials. Before hiring him, they are doing research to see if he is popular with teens. Would they get good survey results from taking a survey about the basketball player from each of these surveys?

1. 200 teens at a basketball game of the basketball player's team

2. 25 teens at a shopping mall

3. 500 students at a number of different middle and high schools

Decide whether each location is a good place to find a representative sample for the selected survey. Justify your answer.

4. number of hours of television watched in a month at a shopping mall

5. favorite kind of entertainment at a movie theater

6. whether families own pets in an apartment complex

7. taste test of a soft drink at a grocery store

8. favorite teacher in a school cafeteria

9. teenagers' favorite magazine at five different high schools

2-9 **Lesson Reading Guide**

Integers and Graphing

Get Ready for the Lesson

Read the introduction at the top of page 121 in your textbook. Write your answers below.

1. What number represents owing 5 dollars? What number represents having 8 dollars left?

2. Who has the most money left? Who owes the most?

Read the Lesson

3. Write an example of a situation that a positive number could represent.

4. Write an example of a situation that a negative number could represent.

5. In the number lines shown in this lesson, how is "continues without end" indicated?

6. How do values change as you move from left to right on a number line?

Remember What You Learned

7. Antonyms are two words that have opposite meanings, such as *cold* and *hot*. Integers can be described by the antonyms *negative* or *positive* or as being *above* zero or *below* zero. Make a table of antonyms that describe situations involving negative and positive integers.

Negative Integer	Positive Integer
loss	gain

Lesson 2–9

2-9 Study Guide and Intervention

Integers and Graphing

Negative numbers represent data that are less than 0. A negative number is written with a − sign. **Positive numbers** represent data that are greater than 0. Positive numbers are written with a + sign or no sign at all.

Opposites are numbers that are the same distance from zero on a number line, but in opposite directions. The set of positive whole numbers, their opposites, and zero are called **integers**.

Example 1 **Write an integer to show 3 degrees below zero. Then graph the integer on a number line.**

Numbers *below zero* are negative numbers. The integer is −3.
Draw a number line. Then draw a dot at the location that represents −3.

```
 +--+--+--●--+--+--+--+--+--+--+--+--+--+
-6 -5 -4 -3 -2 -1  0  1  2  3  4  5  6
```

Example 2 **Make a line plot of the data represented in the table.**

Draw a number line. Put an × above the number that represents each score in the table.

Rachel's Summer Golf Scores

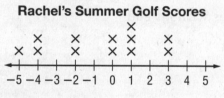

Rachel's Summer Golf Scores			
0	+3	−4	−2
+1	+3	−4	0
+1	−5	−2	+1

Exercises

Write an integer to represent each piece of data. Then graph the integer on the number line.

1. 4 degrees below zero

2. a gain of 2 points

```
 +--+--+--+--+--+--+--+--+--+--+--+--+--+
-6 -5 -4 -3 -2 -1  0  1  2  3  4  5  6
```

3. BOOKS The table shows the change in the ranking from the previous week of the top ten best-selling novels. Make a line plot of the data.

Novel	A	B	C	D	E	F	G	H	I	J
Change in Ranking	+3	−2	0	+1	−2	0	+2	−4	+1	−2

2-9 Skills Practice

Integers and Graphing

Write an integer to represent each piece of data.

1. The football team had a loss of 8 yards on the play.

2. Dewan grew 2 inches last year.

3. The Luther's house is 5 feet above sea level.

4. The book club had a decrease of 6 members since last year.

5. The Panthers scored 10 fewer points than the Bearcats.

6. Jin-Li earned 7 dollars interest in her savings account last month.

7. In the first month, Tyler's puppy gained 5 pounds.

8. The high temperature today was 4 degrees below normal.

Graph each integer on the number line.

```
←—+—+—+—+—+—+—+—+—+—+—+—+—+—+—+—+—+→
  −8  −6  −4  −2   0   2   4   6   8
```

9. 0	10. −3	11. 4	12. +6
13. −5	14. 1	15. −8	16. 7

17. **GAMES** The table shows the number of points C.J. scored on each screen of a computer game. Make a line plot of the data.

Points Scored			
−10	+5	0	−20
+15	+5	+5	−10
0	+10	+5	−15

18. **WEATHER** The table shows the record lowest temperature for 12 different states. Make a line plot of the data.

Record Low Temperature (°F)			
−40	−45	−15	−40
−40	−35	−40	−40
−50	−50	−30	−55

Lesson 2-9

2-9 Practice

Integers and Graphing

Write an integer to represent each situation.

1. Bill drove 25 miles toward Tampa.   2. Susan lost $4.

3. Joe walked down 6 flights of stairs.   4. The baby gained 8 pounds.

Draw a number line from −10 to 10. Then graph each integer on the number line.

5. 2   6. 6   7. 10   8. 8
9. −7   10. −4   11. −9   12. −3

Write the opposite of each integer.

13. +8   14. −5   15. −2   16. +9
17. −11   18. +21   19. +10   20. −7

21. **SCIENCE** The average daytime surface temperature on the Moon is 260°F. Represent this temperature as an integer.

22. **GEOGRAPHY** The Salton Sea is a lake at 227 feet below sea level. Represent this altitude as an integer.

23. **WEATHER** The table below shows the extreme low temperatures for select cities. Make a line plot of the data. Then explain how the line plot can be used to determine whether more cities had extremes lower then zero degrees or greater than zero degrees.

Extreme Low Temperatures by City			
City	Temp. °F	City	Temp. °F
Mobile, AL	3	Boston, MA	−12
Wilmington, DE	−14	Jackson, MS	2
Jacksonville, FL	7	Raleigh, NC	−9
Savannah, GA	3	Portland, OR	−3
New Orleans, LA	11	Philadelphia, PA	−7
Baltimore, MD	−7	Charleston, SC	6

Source: *The World Almanac*

2-9 Word Problem Practice

Integers and Graphing

---

1. MONEY Katryn owes her father $25. Write this number as an integer.

2. GEOGRAPHY Mt. Whitney in California is 14,494 feet above sea level. Write this number as an integer.

---

3. GEOGRAPHY Badwater in Death Valley is 282 feet below sea level. Write this number as an integer.

4. SCHOOL Dick forgot to put his name on his homework. His teacher deducts 5 points for papers turned in without names on them. So, Dick lost 5 points from his score. Write this number as an integer.

---

5. GEOGRAPHY Multnomah Falls in Oregon drops 620 feet from the top to the bottom. Suppose a log is carried by the water from the top to the bottom of the falls. Write the integer to describe the location of the log now.

6. TRAVEL The train left the station and traveled ahead on the tracks for 30 miles. Write an integer to describe the new location of the train from the station.

---

7. WEATHER The table shows the average normal January temperature of three cities in Alaska. Graph the temperatures on a number line.

City	Temperature (°F)
Anchorage	15
Barrow	−13
Fairbanks	−10

8. GAMES The table below shows the number of points Chantal scored on each hand of a card game. Make a line plot of the data.

Points Scored		
+20	+5	0
−5	−10	+5
+5	+10	+10

Lesson 2-9

2-9 Enrichment

Graphs with Integers

Statistical graphs that display temperatures, elevations, and similar data often involve negative quantities. On graphs like these, the scale usually will have a zero point and will include both positive and negative numbers.

For Exercises 1–6, use the bar graph at the right to answer each question.

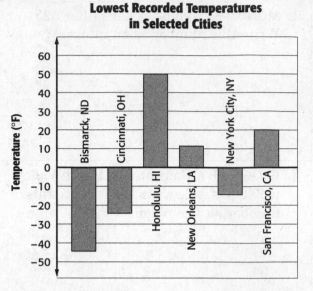

Lowest Recorded Temperatures in Selected Cities

1. In which cities is the record low temperature greater than 0°F?

2. In which cities is the record low temperature less than 0°F?

3. In which city is the record low temperature about −25°F?

4. Estimate the record low temperature for New York City.

5. In which cities is the record low temperature less than twenty degrees from 0°F?

6. How many degrees are between the record low temperatures for Bismarck and Honolulu?

7. In the space at the right, make a bar graph for the data below.

Altitudes of Some California Locations Relative to Sea Level

Location	Altitude (ft)
Alameda	30
Brawley	−112
Calexico	7
Death Valley	−282
El Centro	−39
Salton City	−230

2 Student Recording Sheet

Use this recording sheet with pages 132–133 of the Student Edition.

Part 1: Multiple Choice

Read each question. Then fill in the correct answer.

1. Ⓐ Ⓑ Ⓒ Ⓓ   4. Ⓕ Ⓖ Ⓗ Ⓙ   7. Ⓐ Ⓑ Ⓒ Ⓓ

2. Ⓕ Ⓖ Ⓗ Ⓙ   5. Ⓐ Ⓑ Ⓒ Ⓓ

3. Ⓐ Ⓑ Ⓒ Ⓓ   6. Ⓕ Ⓖ Ⓗ Ⓙ

Part 2: Short Response/Grid in

Record your answer in the blank.

For grid in questions, also enter your answer in the grid by writing each number or symbol in a box. Then fill in the corresponding circle for that number or symbol.

8. _____

9. _____ *(grid in)*

9.

Part 3: Extended Response

Record your answer for Question 10 on the back of this paper.

Assessment

2 Rubric for Scoring Extended Response

SCORE _____

(Use to score the Extended-Response question on page 133 of the Student Edition.)

General Scoring Guidelines

- If a student gives only a correct numerical answer to a problem but does not show how he or she arrived at the answer, the student will be awarded only 1 credit. All extended response questions require the student to show work.

- A fully correct answer for a multiple-part question requires correct responses for all parts of the question. For example, if a question has three parts, the correct response to one or two parts of the question that required work to be shown is *not* considered a fully correct response.

- Students who use trial and error to solve a problem must show their method. Merely showing that the answer checks or is correct is not considered a complete response for full credit.

Exercise 10 Rubric

Score	Specific Criteria
4	An explanation of how the number of credit cards per family is misrepresented is accurate and complete. An explanation of how to change the graph to make it less misleading is accurate and complete.
3	It is noted that the number of credit cards per family is misrepresented, and the explanation of how to change the graph are accurate, but the explanation of why the statement is a misrepresentation is not complete.
2	An explanation of how the number of credit cards per family is misrepresented is accurate and complete, but the explanation of how to change the graph to make it less misleading is inaccurate.
1	It is noted that the number of credit cards per family is misrepresented, but the explanation of why the statement is a misrepresentation is not complete. The explanation of how to change the graph is inaccurate.
0	Response is completely incorrect.

2 Chapter 2 Quiz 1

(Lessons 2-1 through 2-3)

SCHOOL For Questions 1–3, refer to the data below.

1. Make a frequency table of the data.

2. Make a bar graph of the data.

3. Compare the number of students who scored a B to the number who scored an A.

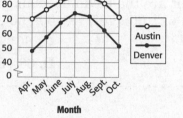

Math Scores

B	B	C	C	A
A	A	B	C	B
C	B	C	B	A
B	B	D	A	B

WEATHER Refer to the line graph.

4. Predict the temperature in Denver and Austin for March.

5. How much warmer would you expect it to be in Austin than in Denver during November?

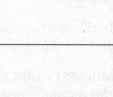

Average Monthly Temperature

1. _____

Students' Math Scores

2. _____

3. _____

4. _____

5. _____

---

2 Chapter 2 Quiz 2

(Lessons 2-4 and 2-5)

1. **SCHOOL** Make a stem-and-leaf plot for the following test scores: 78, 93, 84, 66, 82, 83, 82, 73, 98, 76, 67, 83, 90, 91, 79, and 76.

SHOPPING Refer to the stem-and-leaf plot that shows the costs of bikes at one store.

2. What is the cost of the most expensive bike at the store?

3. How many bikes are less than $140 at the store?

Stem	Leaf
12	0 2 5 5
13	5 9
14	5 5 9

13|5 = $135

SOCCER For Questions 4 and 5, use the table of the number of goals the Eagles scored each game this season.

4. Make a line plot of the data.

Goals Scored Per Game

3	4	1	0	5	2
3	1	2	2	3	6

5. In how many games did the Eagles score 2 goals?

1. _____

2. _____

3. _____

4. _____

5. _____

Assessment

2 Chapter 2 Quiz 3

SCORE _____

(Lessons 2-6 and 2-7)

Find the mean for each set of data.

1. Cost of tennis shoes: $57, $63, $60, $59, $61   1. _____

2. Ages of student's dogs: 5, 6, 3, 4, 8, 10, 6   2. _____

3. **REAL ESTATE** The company shows that their median listing   3.
   is $150,000. If the range of their listings is $50,000, is it
   possible for them to have a house listed for $200,000?   _____
   Explain.

4. Is the median, mode, or mean the most misleading average   4.
   of 4, 92, 96, and 96? Explain.   _____

5. **MULTIPLE-CHOICE** What are the mean, median, and mode of   5. _____
   the temperature data 62°, 60°, 70°, 78°, 60°, 66°, respectively?
   A. 65°, 62°, 60°   **C.** 66°, 64°, 60°
   B. 65°, 64°, 60°   **D.** 66°, 62°, 60°

---

2 Chapter 2 Quiz 4

SCORE _____

(Lessons 2-8 and 2-9)

Select an appropriate type of display for data gathered about each situation.

1. the number of students that chose comedy, drama, horror,   1. _____
   or science fiction as their favorite movie type

2. the number of points Celina scored in each basketball   2. _____
   game this season

3. the change in the daily high temperature over the   3. _____
   past 5 days

For Questions 4–6, write an integer to describe each situation.

4. Move backwards 8 spaces.   4. _____

5. Deposit $25 into an account.   5. _____

6. The temperature outside is 7° below zero.   6. _____

Graph each integer on a number line.

7. −3   8. 0   9. 5   10. −1   7–10.

$$-5 \ -4 \ -3 \ -2 \ -1 \ \ 0 \ \ 1 \ \ 2 \ \ 3 \ \ 4 \ \ 5$$

2 Chapter 2 Mid-Chapter Test

(Lessons 2-1 through 2-5)

PART I

Write the letter for the correct answer in the blank at the right of each question.

GRADES For Questions 1 and 2, refer to the stem-and-leaf plot.

1. How many students scored above a 90 on the math test?

   A. 5   **C.** 9

   B. 6   **D.** 13

Math Test Scores

Stem	Leaf
6	5
7	0 4 4 8
8	0 0 5 5 6 6 9 9
9	1 2 2 4 5
10	0

1. _____

2. Which of the following statements is true?

   F. Five students scored in the 60s.

   G. One student scored below 75.

   H. Three students scored an 85.

   J. Two students scored a 92.

2. _____

For Questions 3 and 4, refer to the line plot.

3. How many students volunteered for 8 hours?

   A. 1   **C.** 3

   B. 2   **D.** 4

Numbered of Hours Students Volunteered

```
              ×   ×
          ×   ×   ×
      ×   ×   ×   ×   ×   ×   ×
      +---+---+---+---+---+---+---+
      7   8   9  10  11  12  13
```

3. _____

4. How many students volunteered for 10 hours or more?

   F. 3   **G.** 4   **H.** 5   **J.** 6

4. _____

PART II

COLLEGE Refer to the table.

5. Make a line graph of the data.

Tuition and Fees at 4-year U.S. Colleges and Institutions	
Year	**Amount ($)**
1980	840
1990	2,159
2000	3,349
2005	4,500

Tuitions and Fees at 4-year U.S. Colleges and Institutions

5.

6. Describe the pattern or trend in the college costs from 1980 to 2005.

6.

_____

Assessment

2 Chapter 2 Vocabulary Test

average	leaves	opposites
bar graph	line graph	outlier
frequency	line plot	positive numbers
graph	mean	range
horizontal axis	median	stem-and-leaf plot
integers	mode	stems
key	negative numbers	vertical axis

Choose the correct term to complete each sentence.

1. The _____ is the middle number, or the mean of the middle two numbers, of the ordered data in a set.

1. _____

2. A _____ is a graph used to compare categories of data.

2. _____

3. The digits written to the left of the vertical rule of a stem-and-leaf plot are called the _____.

3. _____

4. The scale of a vertical bar graph is written on the _____.

4. _____

5. A _____ of a stem-and-leaf plot explains what the stems and leaves represent.

5. _____

6. Extremely high or low values in a data set are called _____.

6. _____

7. The _____ is the number or numbers that occur most frequently in a data set.

7. _____

8. A _____ is a graph used to show how data changes over a period of time.

8. _____

9. A _____ displays data that is ordered from least to greatest and is organized by place value.

9. _____

10. _____ is a common term used to mean a measure of central tendency.

10. _____

In your own words, define each term.

11. range

11. _____

12. mean

12. _____

2 **Chapter 2 Test, Form 1**

TELEVISION **Refer to the frequency table.**

1. What is the most common age of cartoon watchers?

   A. 1–5   **C.** 11–15
   B. 6–10   **D.** 16–20

Cartoon Watchers		
Age	Tally	Frequency
1–5	ẄẄ ẄẄ	10
6–10	ẄẄ ⦀⦀⦀	8
11–15	⦀⦀⦀⦀	4
16–20	ẄẄ ⦀⦀	7

1. _____

2. How many people 11 years or older watched cartoons?

   F. 18   **G.** 19   **H.** 11   **J.** 29

2. _____

ANIMALS **Refer to the bar graph.**

3. Which animal has the same average lifespan as a wolf?

   A. rabbit   **C.** giraffe
   B. horse   **D.** monkey

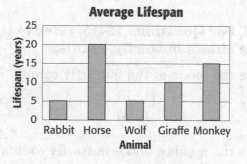

4. Which animal lives twice as long as a giraffe?

   F. rabbit   **H.** wolf
   G. horse   **J.** monkey

3. _____

MONEY **Refer to the line graph.**

5. What was Logan's balance in March?

   A. $100   **C.** $200
   B. $150   **D.** $250

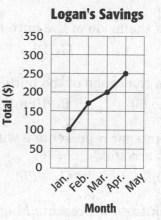

4. _____

6. What is the best prediction for Logan's May balance?

   F. $200   **H.** $300
   G. $250   **J.** $350

5. _____

Refer to the stem-and-leaf plot.

7. What is the greatest number shown in the plot?

   A. 1,044   **C.** 35
   B. 67   **D.** 7

Stem	Leaf
1	0 4 4
2	6 7
3	5

$2\,|\,6 = 26$

6. _____

7. _____

8. How many numbers shown are less than 20?

   F. 0   **G.** 5   **H.** 2   **J.** 3

8. _____

9. How many times is the number 14 shown in the plot?

   A. 0   **B.** 1   **C.** 2   **D.** 3

9. _____

Assessment

2 **Chapter 2 Test, Form 1** *(continued)*

SPORTS Refer to the line plot.

Jeremiah's Points Per Game

10. In how many games did Jeremiah score 8 points?

F. 1   H. 3

G. 2   J. 4

10. _____

11. In how many games did Jeremiah score fewer than 6 points?

A. 1   B. 2   C. 3   D. 4

11. _____

BUTTERFLIES For Questions 12–15, refer to the table that shows Miko's butterfly counts.

Day	Count
Mon.	10
Tues.	13
Wed.	15
Thurs.	52
Fri.	10

12. What is the mean of the butterfly counts?

F. 10   H. 13

G. 12   J. 20

12. _____

13. What is the median of the butterfly counts?

A. 10   B. 12   C. 13   D. 20

13. _____

14. What is the mode of the butterfly counts?

F. 10   G. 12   H. 13   J. 20

14. _____

15. What is the range of the butterfly counts?

A. 10 to 60   B. 10 to 52   C. 42   D. 52

15. _____

16. Which integer represents a withdrawal of $25 from a savings account?

F. -20 G. -25 H. $+20$ J. $+25$

16. _____

17. Which integer represents Maggie earning an allowance of $5?

A. -5 B. 0   C. $+5$ D. $+10$

17. _____

18. Which of the following types of display would be most appropriate to display the change in Terrell's height over the past 5 years?

F. bar graph   H. stem-and-leaf plot

G. line plot   J. line graph

18. _____

Bonus MONEY Sophie's savings usually increases each month. The only time it decreased was in March, when she withdrew some money for a new bike. On a separate sheet of paper, draw a line graph that could show her savings from January through May.

B: _____

2 **Chapter 2 Test, Form 2A**

SCORE _____

SPORTS Refer to the frequency table.

1. What is the interval for the least common number of hours of sports watched?

   A. 1–2   **C.** 5–6
   B. 3–4   **D.** 7–8

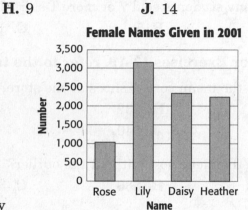

Sports Watchers		
Hours	**Tally**	**Frequency**
1–2	ＩＩＩＩ Ｉ	6
3–4	ＩＩＩＩ ＩＩＩＩ	9
5–6	ＩＩＩＩ	4
7–8	Ｉ	1

1. _____

2. How many people spent 3 or more hours watching sports events?

   F. 5   **G.** 6   **H.** 9   **J.** 14

2. _____

NAMES Refer to the bar graph.

3. What two names shown had about the same popularity?

   A. Lily and Daisy
   B. Daisy and Heather
   C. Lily and Heather
   D. Rose and Daisy

Female Names Given in 2001

3. _____

4. How did the popularity of the name Lily compare with that of Rose?

   F. Rose was given about the same number of times as Lily.

   G. Rose was given about three times more often than Lily.

   H. Lily was given about twice as often as Rose.

   J. Lily was given about three times more often than Rose.

4. _____

MONEY Refer to the line graph.

5. In what month did the greatest increase in sales occur?

   A. January   **C.** March
   B. February   **D.** April

Monthly Sales

5. _____

6. What is the best prediction for June sales?

   F. $2,000   **H.** $2,500
   G. $2,250   **J.** $3,000

6. _____

Use the stem-and-leaf plot.

7. What is the greatest number shown in the plot?

   A. 39   **C.** 79
   B. 38   **D.** 203,779

Stem	Leaf
1	0 7
2	0 3 7 7 9
3	1 8

2 | 3 = 23

7. _____

8. What is the least number shown in the plot?

   F. 0   **G.** 1   **H.** 10   **J.** 107

8. _____

Assessment

2 Chapter 2 Test, Form 2A (continued)

9. How many numbers shown are less than 30?

A. 0   **B.** 2   **C.** 5   **D.** 7   9. _____

FUNDRAISER **Refer to the line plot.**

T-shirts Sold Per Student

10. How many students sold 7 T-shirts?

F. 1   **H.** 3

G. 2   **J.** 4

10. _____

11. How many students sold 7 or more T-shirts?

A. 3   **B.** 5   **C.** 6   **D.** 7   11. _____

SHOPPING **For Exercises 13–19, refer to the table.**

12. What is the mean cost of shoes at the store?

F. $29   **H.** $32

G. $30   **J.** $40

Shoe Costs ($)			
28	40	22	32
40	22	8	40

12. _____

13. What is the mean cost without the outlier?

A. $29   **B.** $30   **C.** $32   **D.** $40   13. _____

14. Which value is the outlier?

F. $8   **G.** $32   **H.** $40   **J.** $22   14. _____

15. What is the median of the data?

A. $29   **B.** $30   **C.** $32   **D.** $40   15. _____

16. What is the mode of the data?

F. $40   **G.** $31   **H.** $22 and $40   **J.** $22   16. _____

17. What is the range of the data?

A. $8   **B.** $1 to $40   **C.** $8 to $40   **D.** $32   17. _____

18. Which integer represents a gain of 7 yards on a play?

F. +7   **G.** +5   **H.** −5   **J.** −7   18. _____

19. Which situation is *not* best described by a negative integer?

A. a withdrawal of $45   **C.** a loss of 12 yards

B. a fine of $15   **D.** a bonus of 10 points   19. _____

20. Which of the following types of display would be most appropriate to display the favorite soft drinks of the sixth grade students?

F. bar graph   **H.** stem-and-leaf plot

G. line plot   **J.** line graph   20. _____

Bonus If three numbers have a mode of 4 and a mean of 5, what are the three numbers?

B: _____

2 Chapter 2 Test, Form 2B

SCORE _____

MUSIC Refer to the frequency table.

1. What is the most common age of music store customers?

   A. 5–8   C. 13–16
   B. 9–12   D. 17–20

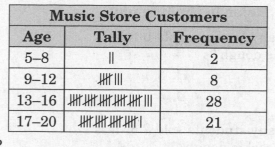

Music Store Customers		
Age	Tally	Frequency
5–8	II	2
9–12	ЖЖ III	8
13–16	ЖЖ ЖЖ ЖЖ ЖЖ ЖЖ III	28
17–20	ЖЖ ЖЖ ЖЖ ЖЖ I	21

1. _____

2. How many people 12 years or younger shopped at the music store?

   F. 2   G. 10   H. 8   J. 49

2. _____

NAMES Refer to the bar graph.

3. What two names shown had about the same popularity?

   A. Rose and Iris
   B. Rosemary and Iris
   C. Violet and Rosemary
   D. Rose and Rosemary

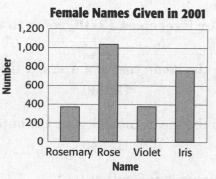

Female Names Given in 2001

3. _____

4. How did the popularity of the name Iris compare with that of Violet?

   F. Violet was given about the same number of times as Iris.
   G. Violet was given about twice as often as Iris.
   H. Iris was given about twice as often as Violet.
   J. Iris was given about three times more often than Violet.

4. _____

MONEY Refer to the line graph.

5. In what month did the greatest decrease in sales occur?

   A. January   C. March
   B. February   D. April

Monthly Sales

5. _____

6. What is the best prediction for June sales?

   F. $500   H. $1,250
   G. $1,000   J. $1,500

6. _____

Use the stem-and-leaf plot.

7. What is the greatest number shown in the plot?

   A. 47   C. 67
   B. 48   D. 323,668

Stem	Leaf
2	0 9
3	2 3 6 6 7
4	1 7

$3|2 = 32$

7. _____

8. What is the least number shown in the plot?

   F. 0   G. 2   H. 20   J. 209

8. _____

9. How many numbers shown are less than 40?

   A. 7   B. 5   C. 2   D. 0

9. _____

Assessment

2 Chapter 2 Test, Form 2B *(continued)*

FUNDRAISER Refer to the line plot.

**Cookie Dough Tubs
Sold Per Student**

10. How many students sold 6 tubs
    of cookie dough?

    F. 1   **H.** 3

    G. 2   **J.** 4

    10. _____

11. How many students sold 7 or less
    tubs of cookie dough?

    A. 3   **B.** 5   **C.** 6   **D.** 7

    11. _____

**SHOPPING For Exercises 13–19, refer to the
table.**

Dress Costs ($)			
38	50	32	42
50	32	10	50

12. What is the mean cost of a dress at the store?

    F. $38   **G.** $40   **H.** $42   **J.** $50

    12. _____

13. What is the mean cost without the outlier?

    A. $38   **B.** $40   **C.** $42   **D.** $50

    13. _____

14. Which value is the outlier?

    F. $38   **G.** $10   **H.** $42   **J.** $50

    14. _____

15. What is the median of the data?

    A. $38   **B.** $40   **C.** $42   **D.** $50

    15. _____

16. What is the mode of the data?

    F. $32   **G.** $40   **H.** $32 and $50   **J.** $50

    16. _____

17. What is the range of the data?

    A. $8   **B.** $40   **C.** $10 to $50   **D.** $52

    17. _____

18. Which integer represents a bonus of 10 points on a math test?

    F. −10   **G.** −5   **H.** +5   **J.** +10

    18. _____

19. Which situation is *not* best described by a negative integer?

    A. a loss of 15 yards   **C.** a decrease of 10 degrees

    B. a deposit of $15   **D.** a penalty of 10 points

    19. _____

20. Which of the following types of display would be most
    appropriate to display the total points the girl's basketball
    team scored in each game this season?

    F. bar graph   **H.** stem-and-leaf plot

    G. line plot   **J.** line graph

    20. _____

Bonus If three numbers have a mode of 3 and a
mean of 5, what are the three numbers?   **B:** _____

2 Chapter 2 Test, Form 2C

VOTING Refer to the table that shows the number of votes cast for Mia (M), Ali (A), Ted (T), and Hattie (H) for best costume.

1. Make a frequency table for the data.

Votes			
H	T	A	H
T	T	H	A
A	A	H	M
A	M	H	H
A	T	A	M

1. _____

2. Who won first place?

2. _____

3. Make a vertical bar graph of the data.

3.
Best Costume

4. How does the number of votes for Hattie compare to votes for Mia?

4. _____
_____

SHOPPING Refer to the table of book costs.

5. Identify the outlier.

Book Costs ($)		
5	5	9
49	11	5

5. _____

6. Find the mean cost of a book at the store. How does the outlier affect the mean?

6. _____
_____

7. The store claims the average item costs $5. Which measure of central tendency are they using to describe the data? Is their claim misleading? Explain.

7. _____
_____

SCHOOL Refer to the table of test scores.

8. Make a stem-and-leaf plot of the data.

Test Scores			
68	73	72	79
81	79	91	87
85	92	95	87
66	87	96	90

8. _____

9. How many students scored 80 or more on the test?

9. _____

10. What is the range of the scores?

10. _____

11. What are the median and mode of the scores?

11. _____

Assessment

CHORES **Refer to the table of weekly allowance.**

Student's Weekly Allowance			
$5	$5	$2	$2
$2	$5	$7	$5
$3	$2	$5	$4
$3	$3	$4	$6

12. Make a line plot of the data.

12.

13. What weekly allowance amount is earned by the most students?

13. _____

MONEY **Ella's savings account balance for January through July was $250, $80, $100, $120, $225, $250, and $275, respectively.**

14. Draw a line graph of Ella's savings for the 7 months.

Ella's Savings

14.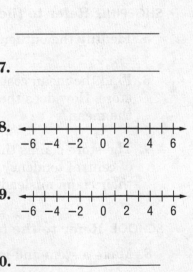

15. Ella bought a stereo, and her savings decreased that month. In which month did she buy the stereo?

15. _____

16. Predict Ella's balance in August. Explain how you made your prediction.

16. _____

_____

17. Write an integer to describe a discount of $10

17. _____

Graph each integer on a number line.

18. −6

18. +—+—+—+—+—+—+—+
    −6 −4 −2 0 2 4 6

19. 5

19. +—+—+—+—+—+—+—+
    −6 −4 −2 0 2 4 6

20. What would be the most appropriate display to show the weight gain of a baby during its first year?

20. _____

Bonus Write a set of nine numbers that has a mean and median of 5.

B: _____

VOTING **Refer to the table that shows the number of votes cast for Miguel (M), Aki (A), Tansy (T), and Hannah (H) for best costume.**

1. Make a frequency table for the data.

Votes				
M	H	T	A	T
H	H	A	T	H
T	T	A	A	T
T	M	A	A	H

1. _____

2. Who won second place?

2. _____

3. Make a vertical bar graph of the data.

3.

Best Costume

4. How does the number of votes for Aki compare to votes for Miguel?

4. _____

_____

SHOPPING **Refer to the table of book costs.**

5. _____

5. Identify the outlier.

Book Costs ($)		
1	1	7
33	1	5

6. Find the mean cost of a book at the store. How does the outlier affect the mean?

6. _____

_____

7. The store claims the average item costs $1. Which measure of central tendency are they using to describe the data? Is their claim misleading? Explain.

7. _____

_____

SCHOOL **Refer to the table of test scores.**

8. Make a stem-and-leaf plot of the data.

Test Scores			
69	95	92	87
72	87	84	78
82	80	68	78
89	78	98	91

8. _____

9. How many students scored 80 or more on the test?

9. _____

10. What is the range of the scores?

10. _____

11. What are the median and mode of the scores?

11. _____

CHORES **Refer to the table of hours students spend doing chores.**

Weekly Hours Spent Doing Chores			
3	4	2	2
5	4	5	1
1	3	5	6
2	3	2	2

12. Make a line plot of the data.

13. What amount of time is spent by the most students doing chores each week?

13. _____

MONEY **Ebony's savings account balance for January through July was $150, $260, $300, $160, $175, $200, and $225, respectively.**

14. Draw a line graph of Ebony's savings for the 7 months.

14. **Ebony's Savings**

15. Ebony bought a stereo, and her savings decreased that month. In which month did she buy the stereo?

15. _____

16. Predict Ebony's balance in August. Explain how you made your prediction.

16. _____

_____

17. Write an integer to describe a bonus of $25.

17. _____

Graph each integer on a number line.

18. −6

18. (number line: −6 −4 −2 0 2 4 6)

19. 5

19. (number line: −6 −4 −2 0 2 4 6)

20. What would be the most appropriate display to show the prices of five different pairs of jeans?

20. _____

Bonus Write a set of seven numbers that has a mean and median of 4.

B: _____

2 Chapter 2 Test, Form 3

SPORTS Refer to the frequency table.

Score	Tally	Frequency
90–99	II	2
100–109	IIII	4
110–119	HHT HHT	10
120–129	IIII	4

1. Twenty students went bowling. How many students scored 100–109 points?

1. _____

2. How many students scored more than 109 points?

2. _____

3. Did anyone score exactly 110 points?

3. _____

_____

WEATHER Refer to the table.

4. Make a bar graph of the data.

Annual Precipitation	
Alaskan City	**Inches**
Bettles	14
Nome	15
King Salmon	20
Yakutat	151
Bethel	15

4. _____

5. Find the mean of the data with and without the outlier.

5. _____

6. What are the mode and median of the data?

6. _____

7. Which measure of central tendency is most misleading?

7. _____

SCHOOL Refer to Luna's test scores shown in the stem-and-leaf plot.

Stem	Leaf
7	7 8 8
8	2 7
9	0

$8|2 = 82$

8. What is the range of her scores?

8. _____

9. Luna can pick which average the teacher will use for her report card. Which one will Luna pick? Explain.

9. _____

_____

DINING Refer to the table of the number of meals families eat out each month.

Number of Meals Out per Month			
5	6	7	2
5	5	8	9
6	5	7	9
6	6	5	4

10. Make a line plot of the data.

10. _____

11. How many families eat out five times each month?

11. _____

Assessment

2 **Chapter 2 Test, Form 3** *(continued)*

INVENTIONS **Refer to the line graph.**

12. Which year had a decrease in the number of patents granted?

12. _____

13. Which year had the greatest increase?

13. _____

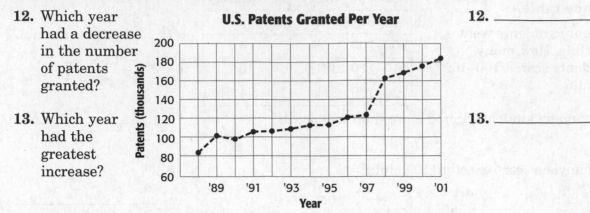

U.S. Patents Granted Per Year

14. Make a stem and leaf plot of the data in the table.

14. _____

Average Number of Lunches Cafeteria Served per Day									
Sept	Oct	Nov	Dec	Jan	Feb	Mar	Apr	May	June
125	120	120	110	118	155	156	156	156	159

Write an integer to describe each situation.

15. Jane lost a twenty dollar bill.

15. _____

16. The balloon expands by three centimeters each second.

16. _____

17. Graph the integer -3 on the number line.

17. _____
-6 -4 -2 0 2 4 6

18. What would be the most appropriate display to show the total points the football team scored in each game this season?

18. _____

19. Write a set of data that has a range of 30, a mode of 68, and a median of 80.

19. _____

20. Which measure of central tendency best describes the data 1, 1, 1, 2, 7, 7, and 9? Explain.

20. _____

_____

Bonus **CODE BREAKING** The table shows the frequencies of the letters used in the original message. Decode the secret message XVKKVKKVOOV.

B: _____

Letter	Freq.
s	4
i	4
p	2
m	1

2 Chapter 2 Extended-Response Test

Demonstrate your knowledge by giving a clear, concise solution to each problem. Be sure to include all relevant drawings and justify your answers. You may show your solution in more than one way or investigate beyond the requirements of the problem. If necessary, record your answer on another piece of paper.

1. Make a frequency table of the data in the table about student grades.

Students' Grades								
A	C	C	B	C	A	C	B	F
B	D	A	C	D	C	D	C	F
C	C	B	B	A	B	C	D	

2. Use your frequency table from Question 1.

   a. Make a bar graph of the data. Be sure to label all the parts of the graph.

   b. Explain how you decided on the scale and interval.

   c. Describe what your graph shows.

   d. How does the number of students with a grade of A compare to the number of students with a grade of D? with a grade of F?

3. Use the bicycle sales data in the table.

   a. Make a line graph of the data in the table about bicycle sales. Be sure to label all the parts of the graph.

   b. Describe the scale and interval. Explain how you decided on them.

   c. Explain what your graph shows.

   d. Describe the change in bicycle sales from 2005 to 2009.

   e. Predict how many bicycles will be sold in 2010. Explain how you decided on your prediction.

Bicycle Sales	
Year	Number (thousands)
2005	10
2006	5
2007	10
2008	15
2009	20

4. Use the test scores at the right.

   a. Make a stem-and-leaf plot of the data in the table of test scores.

   b. Write a sentence that analyzes the data.

   c. Find the mean, median, mode, and range of the data. Show your work.

   d. Identify any outliers and find the mean without the outliers. Describe how the outlier affects the mean of the data.

Scores on a Test					
94	72	82	82	86	66
76	34	98	90	78	92
68	82	76	76	78	84
78	88	84	94	82	80

Assessment

2 **Standardized Test Practice**   SCORE _____

(Chapters 1–2)

Part 1: Multiple Choice

Instructions: Fill in the appropriate circle for the best answer.

---

1. What is the prime factorization of 36? (Lesson 1-2)

   A 2×18 **B** $2 \times 2 \times 9$ **C** 4×9 **D** $2 \times 2 \times 3 \times 3$

   1. Ⓐ Ⓑ Ⓒ Ⓓ

2. Write 8^3 as a product of the same factor. (Lesson 1-3)

   F 8×8 **H** $8 \times 8 \times 8 \times 8$

   G $8 \times 8 \times 8$ **J** $8 \times 8 \times 8 \times 8 \times 8$

   2. Ⓕ Ⓖ Ⓗ Ⓙ

3. Evaluate $3 \times 1 + 7 \times 9$. (Lesson 1-4)

   A 216   **B** 192   **C** 90   **D** 66

   3. Ⓐ Ⓑ Ⓒ Ⓓ

4. Evaluate $2r$ if $r = 37$. (Lesson 1-5)

   F 74   **G** 64   **H** 39   **J** 35

   4. Ⓕ Ⓖ Ⓗ Ⓙ

5. Which equation is true when $q = 7$? (Lesson 1-8)

   A $q + 8 = 16$ **C** $19 - q = 26$

   B $16 = q + 9$ **D** $24 = 16 + q$

   5. Ⓐ Ⓑ Ⓒ Ⓓ

6. What is the area of a rectangle that is 12 inches wide and 13 inches long? (Lesson 1-9)

   F 25 in^2 **G** 50 in^2 **H** 156 in^2 **J** 157 in^2

   6. Ⓕ Ⓖ Ⓗ Ⓙ

7. What are the stems in a stem-and-leaf plot for the data 5, 10, 14, 26, and 34? (Lesson 2-4)

   A 0, 4, 5, 5, 6   **B** 0, 1, 2, 3   **C** 1, 2, 3   **D** 0, 4, 5, 6

   7. Ⓐ Ⓑ Ⓒ Ⓓ

8. How many tennis shoes cost less than $42? (Lesson 2-4)

   F 2

   G 3

   H 4

   J 5

   Tennis Shoe Costs

Stem	Leaf
3	0 5
4	0 2 2 5 8
5	0 5 8
6	5 9

   $4 \,|\, 2 = \$42$

   8. Ⓕ Ⓖ Ⓗ Ⓙ

9. Sasha is buying a new stereo. The range in prices for the stereos she likes is $170. If the most expensive one she likes is $310, how much is the least expensive? (Lesson 2-7)

   A $140   **B** $160   **C** $240   **D** $480

   9. Ⓐ Ⓑ Ⓒ Ⓓ

10. Which data set has a mode of 4? (Lesson 2-7)

    F {1, 2, 3, 4}   **H** {4, 4, 5, 5, 5}

    G {3, 4, 6}   **J** {4, 4, 5}

    10. Ⓕ Ⓖ Ⓗ Ⓙ

2 Standardized Test Practice (continued)

(Chapters 1–2)

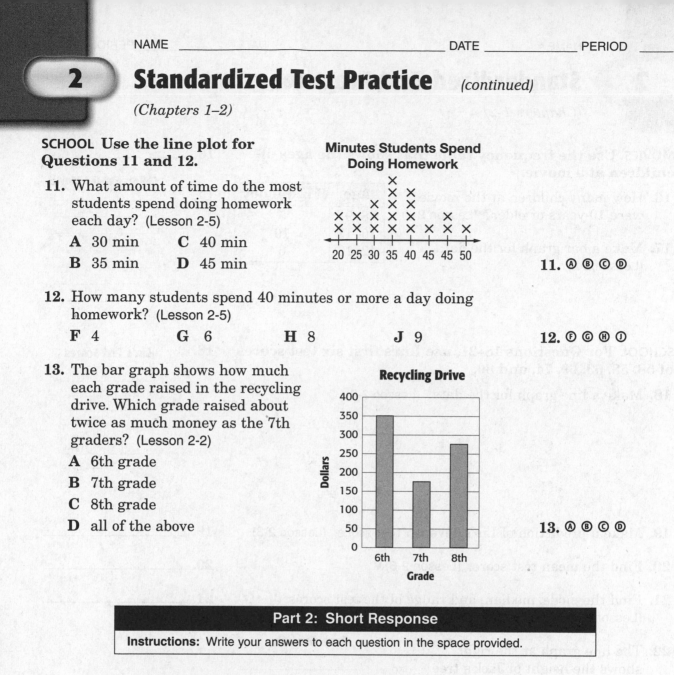

SCHOOL Use the line plot for Questions 11 and 12.

Minutes Students Spend Doing Homework

11. What amount of time do the most students spend doing homework each day? (Lesson 2-5)

   A 30 min   C 40 min

   B 35 min   D 45 min

   11. Ⓐ Ⓑ Ⓒ Ⓓ

12. How many students spend 40 minutes or more a day doing homework? (Lesson 2-5)

   F 4   G 6   H 8   J 9

   12. Ⓕ Ⓖ Ⓗ Ⓘ

13. The bar graph shows how much each grade raised in the recycling drive. Which grade raised about twice as much money as the 7th graders? (Lesson 2-2)

   A 6th grade

   B 7th grade

   C 8th grade

   D all of the above

   Recycling Drive

   13. Ⓐ Ⓑ Ⓒ Ⓓ

Part 2: Short Response

Instructions: Write your answers to each question in the space provided.

14. Tim practiced playing the oboe for 9 minutes on Monday, 13 minutes on Tuesday, and 17 minutes on Wednesday. If he continues to practice in the same pattern, how many minutes will he practice on Thursday? (Lesson 1-1)

   14. _____

15. A store stocks four brands of jeans that cost $18, $20, $24, and $34. What is the mean cost of jeans at the store? (Lesson 2-6)

   15. _____

Assessment

2 ⟩ Standardized Test Practice (continued)

(Chapters 1–2)

MOVIES Use the frequency table that shows the ages of children at a movie.

16. How many children at the movie were 10 years or older? (Lesson 2-2)

17. Make a bar graph for the data. (Lesson 2-2)

Age	Frequency
8–9	5
10–11	10
12–13	6

16. _____

17. _____

Children at the Movie

SCHOOL For Questions 18–21, use Lin's first six test scores of 58, 58, 63, 69, 74, and 80.

18. Make a line graph for the data. (Lesson 2-2)

18.

Lin's Test Scores

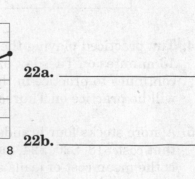

19. Make a prediction of Lin's seventh test score. (Lesson 2-3)

19. _____

20. Find the mean test score. (Lesson 2-6)

20. _____

21. Find the mode, median, and range of the test scores. (Lesson 2-7)

21. _____

22. The line graph at the right shows the height of Jack's tree at the end of each month.

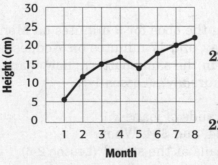

Tree Growth

a. How tall was tree at the end of the third month? (Lesson 2-2)

22a. _____

b. When was the tree about 18 centimeters tall? (Lesson 2-2)

22b. _____

c. One month, Jack trimmed his tree back slightly. Which month was this? (Lesson 2-2)

22c. _____

d. Predict when the tree will reach a height of 26 centimeters. Explain how you made your prediction. (Lesson 2-4)

22d. _____

2 Unit 1 Test

(Chapters 1–2)

1. **SWIMMING** Charmaine swam 2 laps on Monday, 3 laps on Tuesday, 5 laps on Wednesday, and 8 laps on Thursday. If the pattern continues, how many laps will she swim on Friday?

1. _____

Tell whether each number is *prime*, *composite*, or *neither*.

2. 19   3. 28

2. _____

3. _____

Find the prime factorization of each number.

4. 63   5. 36

4. _____

5. _____

Write each product using an exponent. Then find the value of the power.

6. $6 \cdot 6$ 7. $1 \cdot 1 \cdot 1 \cdot 1 \cdot 1$

6. _____

7. _____

Find the value of each expression.

8. $8 + 6 \div 2$ 9. $10 \div 2 + (4^2 - 6)$

8. _____

9. _____

Evaluate each expression if $a = 7$ and $b = 2$.

10. $b + 3$ 11. $a^2 - 4b$

10. _____

11. _____

For Questions 13 and 14, solve each equation mentally.

12. $m + 3 = 19$ 13. $11 = 25 - h$

12. _____

13. _____

14. **AREA** A textbook cover measures 18 centimeters by 24 centimeters. What is the area of the cover of the textbook?

14. _____

SCHOOL Refer to the table.

15. Make a frequency table for the data.

Math Scores			
A	B	A	B
C	B	B	A
B	A	A	A
B	C	B	B
C	A	B	B

15. _____

16. Which score is most common?

16. _____

17. Make a vertical bar graph of the data.

17.

Math Scores

18. Compare the number of students that scored a B to the number that scored a C.

18. _____

Assessment

2 Unit 1 Test (continued)
(Chapters 1–2)

MONEY Eva's savings account balance was $200, $120, $135, $160, and $180 for April through August, respectively.

19. Draw a line graph of Eva's savings for the 5 months.

19.

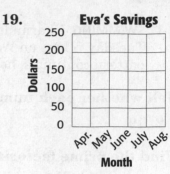

20. In which month did Eva's savings decrease as compared to the savings in the month before?

20. _____

21. Predict Eva's balance in October.

21. _____

CROSS-COUNTRY Refer to the stem-and-leaf plot of the number of miles each member of the cross-country team ran the first week of practice.

Stem	Leaf
0	5 9 9 9
1	1 5 5 5 5 5 5
2	0 0 0 2

$1|5 = 15$ mi

22. What distance did the most members run?

22. _____

23. How many members ran 9 miles?

23. _____

CAFETERIA Refer to the table of the number of times students bought their lunch over the past month.

Lunches Bought in a Month			
7	8	5	4
5	6	7	12
7	8	7	5
9	7	8	6

24. Make a line plot of the data.

24.

25. How many students bought their lunch 5 times over the past month?

25. _____

READING Refer to the table.

Books Read in a Month			
4	25	2	6
3	2	7	

26. What is the mean of the data?

26. _____

27. Which value is the outlier?

27. _____

28. What is the mean without the outlier?

28. _____

29. What is the median number of books read?

29. _____

30. What is the mode of the data?

30. _____

31. What is the range of the data?

31. _____

32. Does the mean, mode, or median best describe the average number of books read? Explain.

32. _____

Answers (Anticipation Guide and Lesson 2-1)

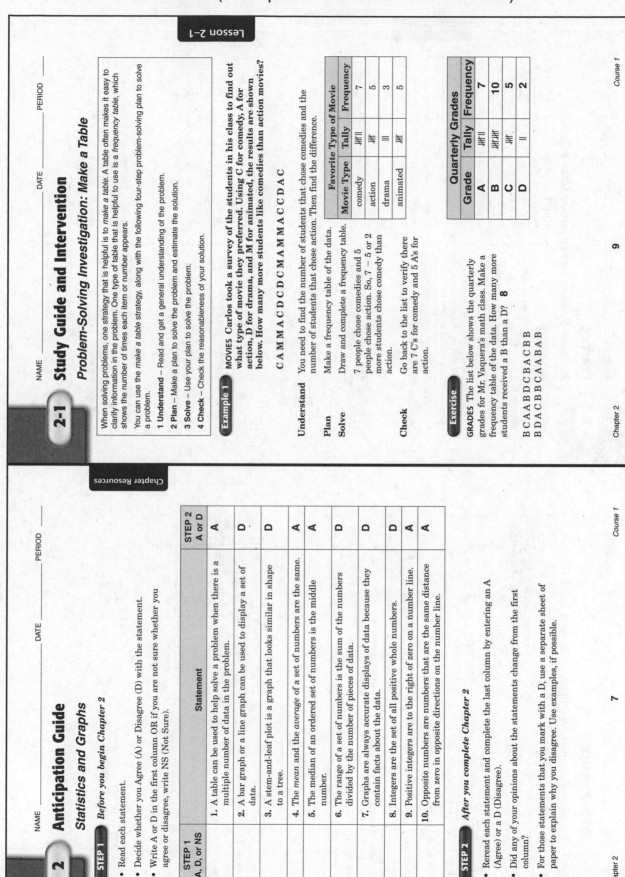

NAME _____ DATE _____ PERIOD _____

2 Anticipation Guide
Statistics and Graphs

STEP 1 *Before you begin Chapter 2*
- Read each statement.
- Decide whether you Agree (A) or Disagree (D) with the statement.
- Write A or D in the first column OR if you are not sure whether you agree or disagree, write NS (Not Sure).

STEP 1 A, D, or NS	Statement	STEP 2 A or D
	1. A table can be used to help solve a problem when there is a multiple number of data in the problem.	A
	2. A bar graph or a line graph can be used to display a set of data.	D
	3. A stem-and-leaf plot is a graph that looks similar in shape to a tree.	D
	4. The *mean* and the *average* of a set of numbers are the same.	A
	5. The median of an ordered set of numbers is the middle number.	A
	6. The range of a set of numbers is the sum of the numbers divided by the number of pieces of data.	D
	7. Graphs are always accurate displays of data because they contain facts about the data.	D
	8. Integers are the set of all positive whole numbers.	D
	9. Positive integers are to the right of zero on a number line.	A
	10. Opposite numbers are numbers that are the same distance from zero in opposite directions on the number line.	A

STEP 2 *After you complete Chapter 2*
- Reread each statement and complete the last column by entering an A (Agree) or a D (Disagree).
- Did any of your opinions about the statements change from the first column?
- For those statements that you mark with a D, use a separate sheet of paper to explain why you disagree. Use examples, if possible.

Chapter 2   7   *Course 1*

NAME _____ DATE _____ PERIOD _____

2-1 Study Guide and Intervention
Problem-Solving Investigation: Make a Table

When solving problems, one strategy that is helpful is to *make a table*. A table often makes it easy to clarify information in the problem. One type of table that is helpful to use is a *frequency table*, which shows the number of times each item or number appears.

You can use the *make a table* strategy, along with the following four-step problem-solving plan to solve a problem.
1 **Understand** – Read and get a general understanding of the problem.
2 **Plan** – Make a plan to solve the problem and estimate the solution.
3 **Solve** – Use your plan to solve the problem.
4 **Check** – Check the reasonableness of your solution.

Example 1 MOVIES Carlos took a survey of the students in his class to find out **what type of movie they preferred. Using C for comedy, A for action, D for drama, and M for animated, the results are shown below. How many more students like comedies than action movies?**

C A M M A C D C D C M A M M A C C D A C

Understand You need to find the number of students that chose comedies and the number of students that chose action. Then find the difference.

Plan Make a frequency table of the data.

Solve Draw and complete a frequency table.

Favorite Type of Movie		
Movie Type	Tally	Frequency
comedy	|||| ||	7
action	||||	5
drama	|||	3
animated	||||	5

7 people chose comedies and 5 people chose action. So, $7 - 5$ or 2 more students chose comedy than action.

Check Go back to the list to verify there are 7 C's for comedy and 5 A's for action.

Exercise GRADES The list below shows the quarterly grades for Mr. Vaquera's math class. Make a frequency table of the data. How many more students received a B than a D? **8**

B C A A B D C B A C B B
B D A C B B C A A B A B

Quarterly Grades		
Grade	Tally	Frequency
A	|||| ||	7
B	|||| ||||	10
C	||||	5
D	||	2

Chapter 2   9   *Course 1*

Chapter 2   A1   *Course 1*

Answers

Answers (Lesson 2-1)

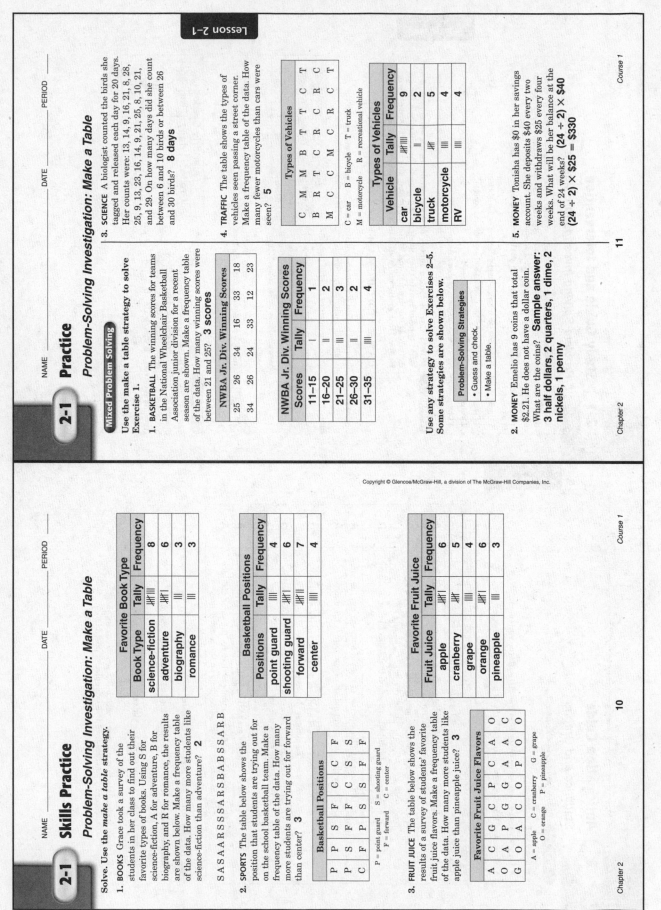

NAME _____ DATE _____ PERIOD _____

2-1 Practice

Problem-Solving Investigation: Make a Table

Mixed Problem Solving

Use the make a table strategy to solve Exercise 1.

1. **BASKETBALL** The winning scores for teams in the National Wheelchair Basketball Association junior division for a recent season are shown below. Make a frequency table of the data. How many winning scores were between 21 and 25? **3 scores**

NWBA Jr. Div. Winning Scores

25	26	34	16	33	18
34	26	24	33	12	23

NWBA Jr. Div. Winning Scores

Scores	Tally	Frequency
11–15	I	1
16–20	II	2
21–25	III	3
26–30	II	2
31–35	IIII	4

Use any strategy to solve Exercises 2–5. Some strategies are shown below.

Problem-Solving Strategies
- Guess and check.
- Make a table.

2. **MONEY** Emelio has 9 coins that total $2.21. He does not have a dollar coin. What are the coins? **Sample answer: 3 half dollars, 2 quarters, 1 dime, 2 nickels, 1 penny**

3. **SCIENCE** A biologist counted the birds she tagged and released each day for 20 days. Her counts were: 13, 14, 9, 16, 21, 8, 28, 25, 9, 13, 23, 16, 14, 9, 21, 25, 8, 10, 21, and 29. On how many days did she count between 6 and 10 birds or between 26 and 30 birds? **8 days**

4. **TRAFFIC** The table shows the types of vehicles seen passing a street corner. Make a frequency table of the data. How many fewer motorcycles than cars were seen? **5**

Types of Vehicles

C	M	M	B	T	T	C	T
B	R	T	C	R	C	R	C
M	C	C	M	C	R	C	T

C = car   B = bicycle   T = truck
M = motorcycle   R = recreational vehicle

Types of Vehicles

Vehicle	Tally	Frequency
car	IIIII IIII	9
bicycle	II	2
truck	IIIII	5
motorcycle	IIII	4
RV	IIII	4

5. **MONEY** Tonisha has $0 in her savings account. She deposits $40 every two weeks and withdraws $25 every four weeks. What will be her balance at the end of 24 weeks? $(24 \div 2) \times \$40$ $(24 \div 2) \times \$25 = \$330$ $(24 \div 2) \times \$40$ **$40**

Chapter 2   11   Course 1

NAME _____ DATE _____ PERIOD _____

2-1 Skills Practice

Problem-Solving Investigation: Make a Table

Solve. Use the make a table strategy.

1. **BOOKS** Grace took a survey of the students in her class to find out their favorite types of books. Using S for science-fiction, A for adventure, B for biography, and R for romance, the results are shown below. Make a frequency table of the data. How many more students like science-fiction than adventure? **2**

S A S A A R S S S A R S B A B S S A A R B

Favorite Book Type

Book Type	Tally	Frequency
science-fiction	IIIII III	8
adventure	IIIII I	6
biography	III	3
romance	III	3

2. **SPORTS** The table below shows the position that students are trying out for on the school basketball team. Make a frequency table of the data. How many more students are trying out for forward than center? **3**

Basketball Positions

P	P	S	F	F	C	C	F
P	S	F	F	C	S	S	F
C	F	P	S	S	F	F	

P = point guard   S = shooting guard
F = forward   C = center

Basketball Positions

Positions	Tally	Frequency
point guard	IIII	4
shooting guard	IIIII I	6
forward	IIIII II	7
center	IIII	4

3. **FRUIT JUICE** The table below shows the results of a survey of students' favorite fruit juice flavors. Make a frequency table of the data. How many more students like apple juice than pineapple juice? **3**

Favorite Fruit Juice Flavors

A	C	G	C	P	C	A	O
O	A	P	G	G	A	A	C
G	O	A	C	O	P	O	O

A = apple   C = cranberry   G = grape
O = orange   P = pineapple

Favorite Fruit Juice

Fruit Juice	Tally	Frequency
apple	IIIII I	6
cranberry	IIIII	5
grape	IIII	4
orange	IIIII I	6
pineapple	III	3

Chapter 2   10   Course 1

Answers (Lessons 2-1 and 2-2)

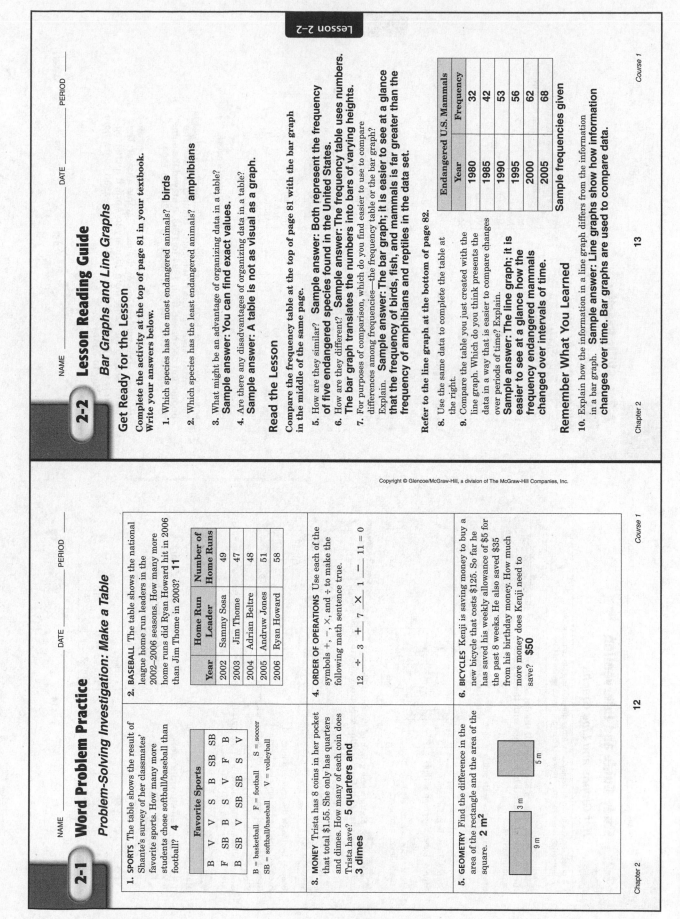

NAME _____ DATE _____ PERIOD _____

2-1 Word Problem Practice

Problem-Solving Investigation: Make a Table

1. **SPORTS** The table shows the result of Shante's survey of her classmates' favorite sports. How many more students chose softball/baseball than football? **4**

Favorite Sports				
B	V	V	S	B
F	SB	B	S	V
B	SB	V	SB	SB
	SB		S	V

SB | SB
F | B
SB | V

B = basketball   F = football   S = soccer
SB = softball/baseball   V = volleyball

2. **BASEBALL** The table shows the national league home run leaders in the 2002–2006 seasons. How many more home runs did Ryan Howard hit in 2006 than Jim Thome in 2003? **11**

Year	Home Run Leader	Number of Home Runs
2002	Sammy Sosa	49
2003	Jim Thome	47
2004	Adrian Beltre	48
2005	Andruw Jones	51
2006	Ryan Howard	58

3. **MONEY** Trista has 8 coins in her pocket that total $1.55. She only has quarters and dimes. How many of each coin does Trista have? **5 quarters and 3 dimes**

4. **ORDER OF OPERATIONS** Use each of the symbols $+$, $-$, $\times$, and $\div$ to make the following math sentence true.

$12 \;\underline{\div}\; 3 \;\underline{+}\; 7 \;\underline{\times}\; 1 \;\underline{-}\; 11 = 0$

5. **GEOMETRY** Find the difference in the area of the rectangle and the area of the square. **2 m²**

9 m
3 m

5 m

6. **BICYCLES** Kenji is saving money to buy a new bicycle that costs $125. So far he has saved his weekly allowance of $5 for the past 8 weeks. He also saved $35 from his birthday money. How much more money does Kenji need to save? **$50**

NAME _____ DATE _____ PERIOD _____

2-2 Lesson Reading Guide

Bar Graphs and Line Graphs

Get Ready for the Lesson

Complete the activity at the top of page 81 in your textbook. Write your answers below.

1. Which species has the most endangered animals? **birds**

2. Which species has the least endangered animals? **amphibians**

3. What might be an advantage of organizing data in a table? **Sample answer: You can find exact values.**

4. Are there any disadvantages of organizing data in a table? **Sample answer: A table is not as visual as a graph.**

Read the Lesson

Compare the frequency table at the top of page 81 with the bar graph in the middle of the same page.

5. How are they similar? **Sample answer: Both represent the frequency of five endangered species found in the United States.**

6. How are they different? **Sample answer: The frequency table uses numbers. The bar graph translates the numbers into bars of varying heights.**

7. For purposes of comparison, which do you find easier to use to compare differences among frequencies—the frequency table or the bar graph? Explain. **Sample answer: The bar graph; it is easier to see at a glance that the frequency of birds, fish, and mammals is far greater than the frequency of amphibians and reptiles in the data set.**

Refer to the line graph at the bottom of page 82.

8. Use the same data to complete the table at the right.

Endangered U.S. Mammals	
Year	Frequency
1980	32
1985	42
1990	53
1995	56
2000	62
2005	68

Sample frequencies given

9. Compare the table you just created with the line graph. Which do you think presents the data in a way that is easier to compare changes over periods of time? Explain. **Sample answer: The line graph; it is easier to see at a glance how the frequency endangered mammals changed over intervals of time.**

Remember What You Learned

10. Explain how the information in a line graph differs from the information in a bar graph. **Sample answer: Line graphs show how information changes over time. Bar graphs are used to compare data.**

Lesson 2-2

Answers

Answers (Lesson 2-2)

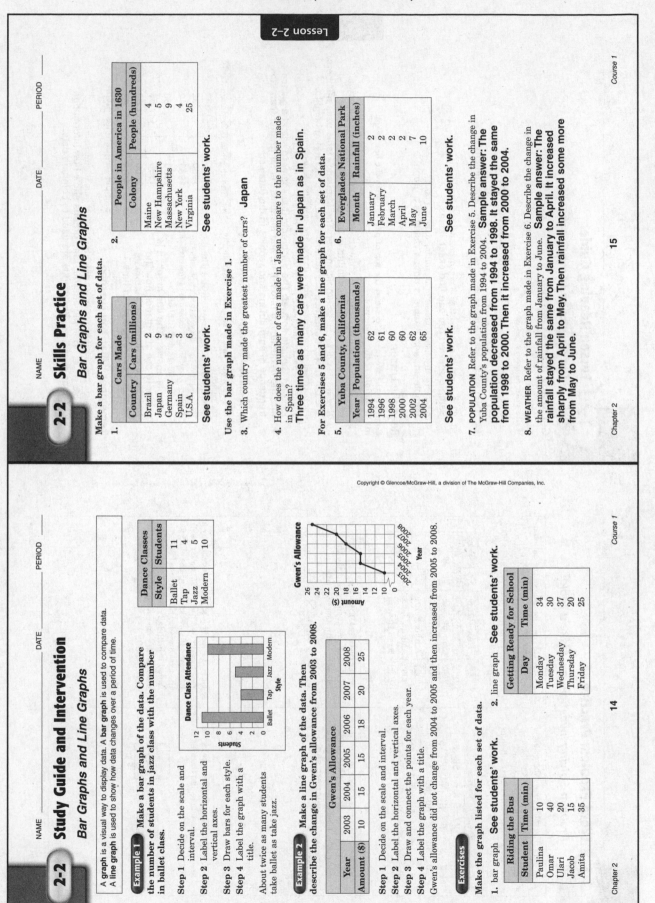

2-2 Study Guide and Intervention

NAME _____ DATE _____ PERIOD _____

Bar Graphs and Line Graphs

A **graph** is a visual way to display data. A **bar graph** is used to compare data.
A **line graph** is used to show how data changes over a period of time.

Example 1 Make a bar graph of the data. Compare the number of students in jazz class with the number in ballet class.

Dance Classes	
Style	Students
Ballet	11
Tap	4
Jazz	5
Modern	10

Step 1 Decide on the scale and interval.

Step 2 Label the horizontal and vertical axes.

Step 3 Draw bars for each style.

Step 4 Label the graph with a title.

About twice as many students take ballet as take jazz.

Dance Class Attendance (bar graph showing Students vs Style: Ballet, Tap, Jazz, Modern)

Example 2 Make a line graph of the data. Then describe the change in Gwen's allowance from 2003 to 2008.

Gwen's Allowance						
Year	2003	2004	2005	2006	2007	2008
Amount ($)	10	15	15	18	20	25

Step 1 Decide on the scale and interval.

Step 2 Label the horizontal and vertical axes.

Step 3 Draw and connect the points for each year.

Step 4 Label the graph with a title.

Gwen's allowance did not change from 2004 to 2005 and then increased from 2005 to 2008.

(Line graph: Gwen's Allowance, Amount ($) vs Year 2003–2008)

Exercises

Make the graph listed for each set of data.

1. bar graph   **See students' work.**

Riding the Bus	
Student	Time (min)
Paulina	10
Omar	40
Ulari	20
Jacob	15
Amita	35

2. line graph   **See students' work.**

Getting Ready for School	
Day	Time (min)
Monday	34
Tuesday	30
Wednesday	37
Thursday	20
Friday	25

2-2 Skills Practice

NAME _____ DATE _____ PERIOD _____

Bar Graphs and Line Graphs

Make a bar graph for each set of data.

1.

Cars Made	
Country	Cars (millions)
Brazil	2
Japan	9
Germany	5
Spain	3
U.S.A.	6

See students' work.

2.

People in America in 1630	
Colony	People (hundreds)
Maine	4
New Hampshire	5
Massachusetts	9
New York	4
Virginia	25

See students' work.

Use the bar graph made in Exercise 1.

3. Which country made the greatest number of cars? **Japan**

4. How does the number of cars made in Japan compare to the number made in Spain? **Three times as many cars were made in Japan as in Spain.**

For Exercises 5 and 6, make a line graph for each set of data.

5.

Yuba County, California	
Year	Population (thousands)
1994	62
1996	61
1998	60
2000	60
2002	62
2004	65

See students' work.

6.

Everglades National Park	
Month	Rainfall (inches)
January	2
February	2
March	2
April	2
May	7
June	10

See students' work.

7. POPULATION Refer to the graph made in Exercise 5. Describe the change in Yuba County's population from 1994 to 2004. **Sample answer: The population decreased from 1994 to 1998. It stayed the same from 1998 to 2000. Then it increased from 2000 to 2004.**

8. WEATHER Refer to the graph made in Exercise 6. Describe the change in the amount of rainfall from January to June. **Sample answer: The rainfall stayed the same from January to April. It increased sharply from April to May. Then rainfall increased some more from May to June.**

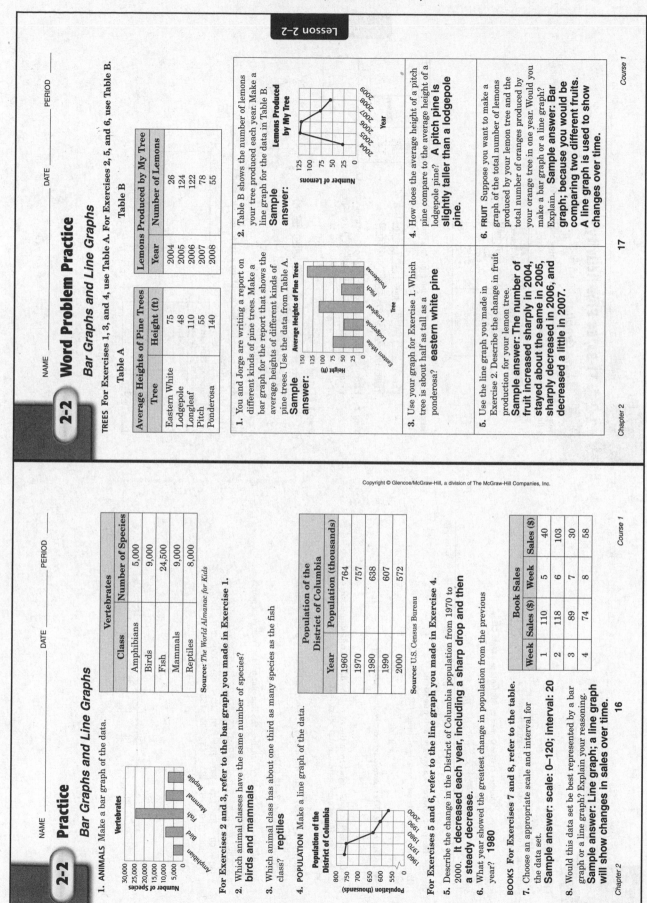

Lesson 2-2

2-2 Word Problem Practice

Bar Graphs and Line Graphs

TREES For Exercises 1, 3, and 4, use Table A. For Exercises 2, 5, and 6, use Table B.

Table A

Average Heights of Pine Trees	
Tree	Height (ft)
Eastern White	75
Lodgepole	48
Longleaf	110
Pitch	55
Ponderosa	140

Table B

Lemons Produced by My Tree	
Year	Number of Lemons
2004	26
2005	124
2006	122
2007	78
2008	55

1. You and Jorge are writing a report on different kinds of pine trees. Make a bar graph for the report that shows the average heights of different kinds of pine trees. Use the data from Table A. **Sample answer:**

2. Table B shows the number of lemons your tree produced each year. Make a line graph for the data in Table B. **Sample answer:**

3. Use your graph for Exercise 1. Which tree is about half as tall as a ponderosa? **eastern white pine**

4. How does the average height of a pitch pine compare to the average height of a lodgepole pine? **A pitch pine is slightly taller than a lodgepole pine.**

5. Use the line graph you made in Exercise 2. Describe the change in fruit production for your lemon tree. **Sample answer: The number of fruit increased sharply in 2004, stayed about the same in 2005, sharply decreased in 2006, and decreased a little in 2007.**

6. **FRUIT** Suppose you want to make a graph of the total number of lemons produced by your lemon tree and the total number of oranges produced by your orange tree in one year. Would you make a bar graph or a line graph? Explain. **Sample answer: Bar graph; because you would be comparing two different fruits. A line graph is used to show changes over time.**

Chapter 2 17 *Course 1*

2-2 Practice

Bar Graphs and Line Graphs

1. **ANIMALS** Make a bar graph of the data.

Vertebrates	
Class	Number of Species
Amphibians	5,000
Birds	9,000
Fish	24,500
Mammals	9,000
Reptiles	8,000

Source: *The World Almanac for Kids*

For Exercises 2 and 3, refer to the bar graph you made in Exercise 1.

2. Which animal classes have the same number of species? **birds and mammals**

3. Which animal class has about one third as many species as the fish class? **reptiles**

4. **POPULATION** Make a line graph of the data.

Population of the District of Columbia	
Year	Population (thousands)
1960	764
1970	757
1980	638
1990	607
2000	572

Source: U.S. Census Bureau

For Exercises 5 and 6, refer to the line graph you made in Exercise 4.

5. Describe the change in the District of Columbia population from 1970 to 2000. **It decreased each year, including a sharp drop and then a steady decrease.**

6. What year showed the greatest change in population from the previous year? **1980**

BOOKS For Exercises 7 and 8, refer to the table.

Book Sales			
Week	Sales ($)	Week	Sales ($)
1	110	5	40
2	118	6	103
3	89	7	30
4	74	8	58

7. Choose an appropriate scale and interval for the data set. **Sample answer: scale: 0–120; interval: 20**

8. Would this data set be best represented by a bar graph or a line graph? Explain your reasoning. **Sample answer: Line graph; a line graph will show changes in sales over time.**

Chapter 2 16 *Course 1*

Answers

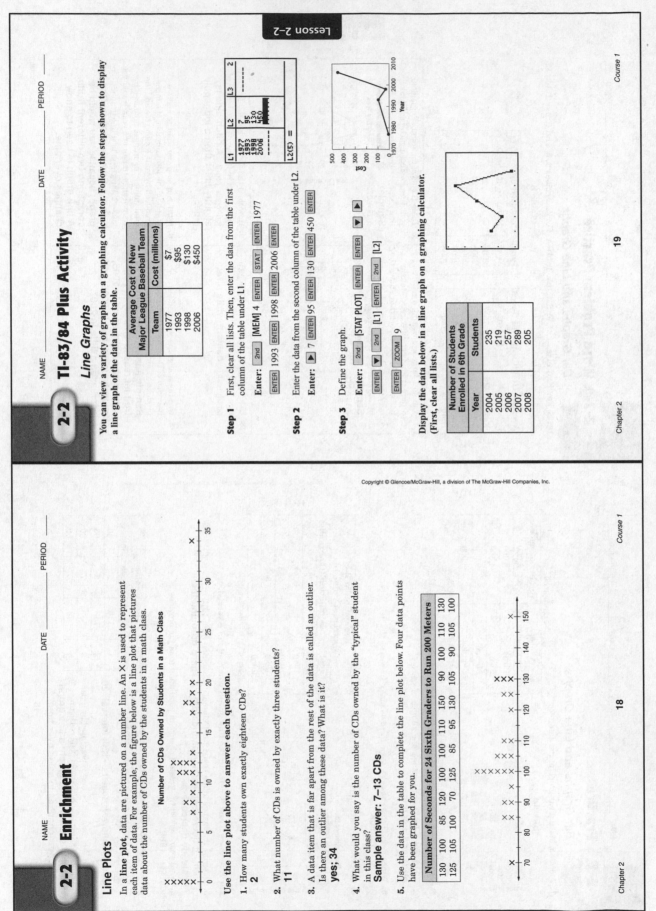

Lesson 2-2

NAME _____ DATE _____ PERIOD _____

2-2 TI-83/84 Plus Activity

Line Graphs

You can view a variety of graphs on a graphing calculator. Follow the steps shown to display a line graph of the data in the table.

Average Cost of New Major League Baseball Team

Team	Cost (millions)
1977	$7
1993	$95
1998	$130
2006	$450

Step 1 First, clear all lists. Then, enter the data from the first column of the table under L1.

Enter: 2nd [MEM] 4 ENTER STAT ENTER 1977 ENTER 1993 ENTER 1998 ENTER 2006 ENTER

Step 2 Enter the data from the second column of the table under L2.

Enter: ▲ 7 ENTER 95 ENTER 130 ENTER 450 ENTER

Step 3 Define the graph.

Enter: 2nd [STAT PLOT] ENTER ENTER ▲ ENTER ▶ ENTER ▶ 2nd [L1] ENTER 2nd [L2] ENTER ZOOM 9

Display the data below in a line graph on a graphing calculator. (First, clear all lists.)

Number of Students Enrolled in 6th Grade

Year	Students
2004	235
2005	219
2006	257
2007	289
2008	205

Chapter 2   19   *Course 1*

NAME _____ DATE _____ PERIOD _____

2-2 Enrichment

Line Plots

In a **line plot**, data are pictured on a number line. An X is used to represent each item of data. For example, the figure below is a line plot that pictures data about the number of CDs owned by the students in a math class.

Number of CDs Owned by Students in a Math Class

Use the line plot above to answer each question.

1. How many students own exactly eighteen CDs?
   2

2. What number of CDs is owned by exactly three students?
   11

3. A data item that is far apart from the rest of the data is called an outlier. Is there an outlier among these data? What is it?
   yes; 34

4. What would you say is the number of CDs owned by the "typical" student in this class?
   Sample answer: 7–13 CDs

5. Use the data in the table to complete the line plot below. Four data points have been graphed for you.

Number of Seconds for 24 Sixth Graders to Run 200 Meters

130	100	85	120	100	100	110	150	90	100	110	130
125	105	100	70	125	95	130	105	90	105	100	

Chapter 2   18   *Course 1*

Chapter 2   **A6**   *Course 1*

Answers (Lesson 2-3)

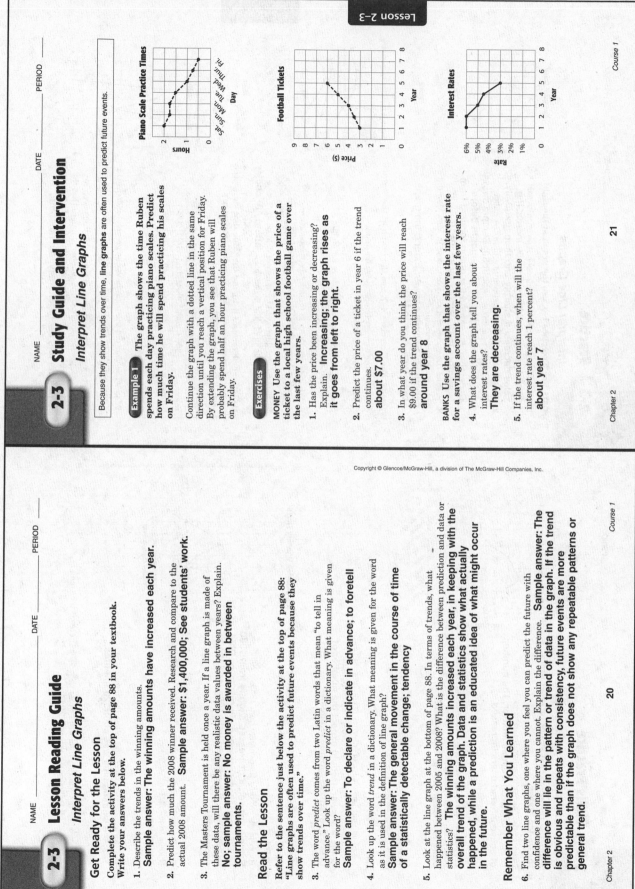

NAME _____ DATE _____ PERIOD _____

2-3 Study Guide and Intervention

Interpret Line Graphs

Because they show trends over time, line graphs are often used to predict future events.

Example 1 The graph shows the time Ruben spends each day practicing piano scales. Predict how much time he will spend practicing his scales on Friday.

Continue the graph with a dotted line in the same direction until you reach a vertical position for Friday. By extending the graph, you see that Ruben will probably spend half an hour practicing piano scales on Friday.

Piano Scale Practice Times

Exercises

MONEY Use the graph that shows the price of a ticket to a local high school football game over the last few years.

1. Has the price been increasing or decreasing? Explain. **Increasing; the graph rises as it goes from left to right.**

2. Predict the price of a ticket in year 6 if the trend continues. **about $7.00**

3. In what year do you think the price will reach $9.00 if the trend continues? **around year 8**

Football Tickets

BANKS Use the graph that shows the interest rate for a savings account over the last few years.

4. What does the graph tell you about interest rates? **They are decreasing.**

5. If the trend continues, when will the interest rate reach 1 percent? **about year 7**

Interest Rates

Chapter 2   21   Course 1

NAME _____ DATE _____ PERIOD _____

2-3 Lesson Reading Guide

Interpret Line Graphs

Get Ready for the Lesson

Complete the activity at the top of page 88 in your textbook. Write your answers below.

1. Describe the trends in the winning amounts. **Sample answer: The winning amounts have increased each year.**

2. Predict how much the 2008 winner received. Research and compare to the actual 2008 amount. **Sample answer: $1,400,000; See students' work.**

3. The Masters Tournament is held once a year. If a line graph is made of these data, will there be any realistic data values between years? Explain. **No; sample answer: No money is awarded in between tournaments.**

Read the Lesson

Refer to the sentence just below the activity at the top of page 88: "Line graphs are often used to predict future events because they show trends over time."

3. The word *predict* comes from two Latin words that mean "to tell in advance." Look up the word *predict* in a dictionary. What meaning is given for the word? **Sample answer: To declare or indicate in advance; to foretell**

4. Look up the word *trend* in a dictionary. What meaning is given for the word as it is used in the definition of line graph? **Sample answer: The general movement in the course of time of a statistically detectable change; tendency**

5. Look at the line graph at the bottom of page 88. In terms of trends, what happened between 2005 and 2008? What is the difference between prediction and data or statistics? **The winning amounts increased each year, in keeping with the overall trend of the graph. Data and statistics show what actually happened, while a prediction is an educated idea of what might occur in the future.**

Remember What You Learned

6. Find two line graphs, one where you feel you can predict the future with confidence and one where you cannot. Explain the difference. **Sample answer: The difference will lie in the pattern or trend of data in the graph. If the trend is obvious and repeats with consistency, future events are more predictable than if the graph does not show any repeatable patterns or general trend.**

Chapter 2   20   Course 1

Answers

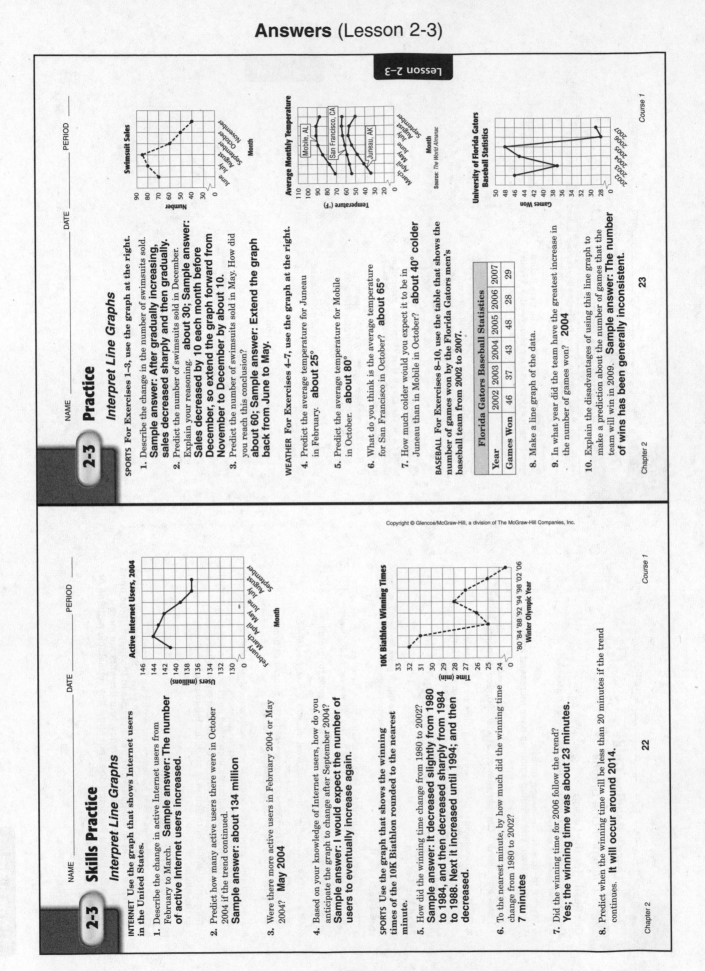

NAME _____ DATE _____ PERIOD _____

2-3 Practice

Interpret Line Graphs

SPORTS For Exercises 1–3, use the graph at the right.

Swimsuit Sales

1. Describe the change in the number of swimsuits sold. **Sample answer: After gradually increasing, sales decreased sharply and then gradually.**

2. Predict the number of swimsuits sold in December. **about 30; Sample answer: Sales decreased by 10 each month before December, so extend the graph forward from November to December by about 10.** Explain your reasoning.

3. Predict the number of swimsuits sold in May. How did you reach this conclusion? **about 60; Sample answer: Extend the graph back from June to May.**

WEATHER For Exercises 4–7, use the graph at the right.

Average Monthly Temperature

4. Predict the average temperature for Juneau in February. **about 25°**

5. Predict the average temperature for Mobile in October. **about 80°**

6. What do you think is the average temperature for San Francisco in October? **about 65°**

7. How much colder would you expect it to be in Juneau than in Mobile in October? **about 40° colder**

BASEBALL For Exercises 8–10, use the table that shows the number of games won by the Florida Gators men's baseball team from 2002 to 2007.

Florida Gators Baseball Statistics

Year	2002	2003	2004	2005	2006	2007
Games Won	46	37	43	48	28	29

8. Make a line graph of the data.

University of Florida Gators Baseball Statistics

9. In what year did the team have the greatest increase in the number of games won? **2004**

10. Explain the disadvantages of using this line graph to make a prediction about the number of games that the team will win in 2009. **Sample answer: The number of wins has been generally inconsistent.**

Chapter 2   23   Course 1

NAME _____ DATE _____ PERIOD _____

2-3 Skills Practice

Interpret Line Graphs

INTERNET Use the graph that shows Internet users in the United States.

Active Internet Users, 2004

1. Describe the change in active Internet users from February to March. **Sample answer: The number of active Internet users increased.**

2. Predict how many active users there were in October 2004 if the trend continued. **Sample answer: about 134 million**

3. Were there more active users in February 2004 or May 2004? **May 2004**

4. Based on your knowledge of Internet users, how do you anticipate the graph to change after September 2004? **Sample answer: I would expect the number of users to eventually increase again.**

SPORTS Use the graph that shows the winning times of the 10K Biathlon rounded to the nearest minute.

10K Biathlon Winning Times

5. How did the winning time change from 1980 to 2002? **Sample answer: It decreased slightly from 1980 to 1984, and then decreased sharply from 1984 to 1988. Next it increased until 1994; and then decreased.**

6. To the nearest minute, by how much did the winning time change from 1980 to 2002? **7 minutes**

7. Did the winning time for 2006 follow the trend? **Yes; the winning time was about 23 minutes.**

8. Predict when the winning time will be less than 20 minutes if the trend continues. **It will occur around 2014.**

Chapter 2   22   Course 1

Answers (Lesson 2-3)

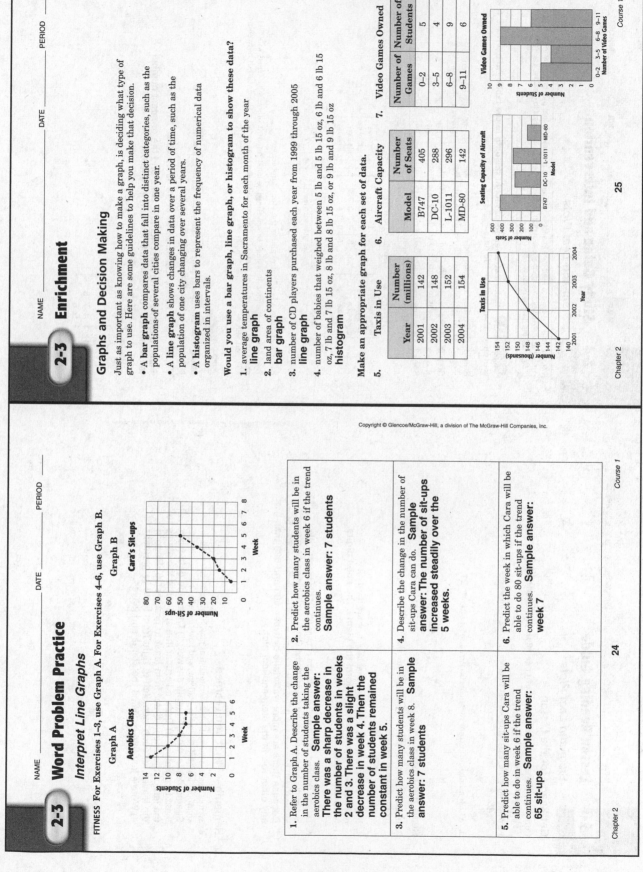

NAME _____ DATE _____ PERIOD _____

2-3 Enrichment

Graphs and Decision Making

Just as important as knowing how to make a graph, is deciding what type of graph to use. Here are some guidelines to help you make that decision.

- A **bar graph** compares data that fall into distinct categories, such as the populations of several cities compare in one year.
- A **line graph** shows changes in data over a period of time, such as the population of one city changing over several years.
- A **histogram** uses bars to represent the frequency of numerical data organized in intervals.

Would you use a bar graph, line graph, or histogram to show these data?

1. average temperatures in Sacramento for each month of the year
   line graph

2. land area of continents
   bar graph

3. number of CD players purchased each year from 1999 through 2005
   line graph

4. number of babies that weighed between 5 lb and 5 lb 15 oz, 6 lb and 6 lb 15 oz, 7 lb and 7 lb 15 oz, 8 lb and 8 lb 15 oz, or 9 lb and 9 lb 15 oz
   histogram

Make an appropriate graph for each set of data.

5. **Taxis in Use**

Year	Number (millions)
2001	142
2002	148
2003	152
2004	154

6. **Aircraft Capacity**

Model	Number of Seats
B747	405
DC-10	288
L-1011	296
MD-80	142

7. **Video Games Owned**

Number of Games	Number of Students
0–2	5
3–5	4
6–8	9
9–11	6

NAME _____ DATE _____ PERIOD _____

2-3 Word Problem Practice

Interpret Line Graphs

FITNESS For Exercises 1–3, use Graph A. For Exercises 4–6, use Graph B.

1. Refer to Graph A. Describe the change in the number of students taking the aerobics class. **Sample answer: There was a sharp decrease in the number of students in weeks 2 and 3. There was a slight decrease in week 4. Then the number of students remained constant in week 5.**

2. Predict how many students will be in the aerobics class in week 6 if the trend continues. **Sample answer: 7 students**

3. Predict how many students will be in the aerobics class in week 8. **Sample answer: 7 students**

4. Describe the change in the number of sit-ups Cara can do. **Sample answer: The number of sit-ups increased steadily over the 5 weeks.**

5. Predict how many sit-ups Cara will be able to do in week 6 if the trend continues. **Sample answer: 65 sit-ups**

6. Predict the week in which Cara will be able to do 80 sit-ups if the trend continues. **Sample answer: week 7**

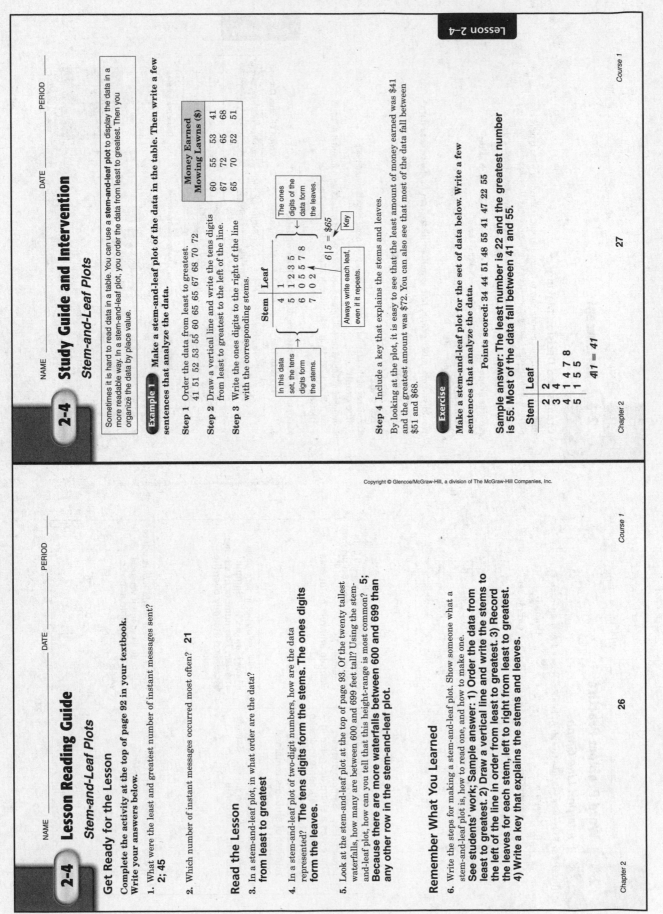

2-4 Study Guide and Intervention

NAME _____ DATE _____ PERIOD _____

Stem-and-Leaf Plots

Sometimes it is hard to read data in a table. You can use a **stem-and-leaf plot** to display the data in a more readable way. In a stem-and-leaf plot, you order the data from least to greatest. Then you organize the data by place value.

Example 1 **Make a stem-and-leaf plot of the data in the table. Then write a few sentences that analyze the data.**

Money Earned Mowing Lawns ($)			
60	55	53	41
67	72	65	68
65	70	52	51

Step 1 Order the data from least to greatest.
41 51 52 53 55 60 65 65 67 68 70 72

Step 2 Draw a vertical line and write the tens digits from least to greatest to the left of the line.

Step 3 Write the ones digits to the right of the line with the corresponding stems.

Stem	Leaf
4	1
5	1 2 3 5
6	0 5 5 7 8
7	0 2

$6|5 = \$65$ Key

In this data set, the tens digits form the stems.

The ones digits of the data form the leaves.

Always write each leaf, even if it repeats.

Step 4 Include a key that explains the stems and leaves.
By looking at the plot, it is easy to see that the least amount of money earned was $41 and the greatest amount was $72. You can also see that most of the data fall between $51 and $68.

Exercise

Make a stem-and-leaf plot for the set of data below. Write a few sentences that analyze the data.

Points scored: 34 44 51 48 55 41 47 22 55

Sample answer: The least number is 22 and the greatest number is 55. Most of the data fall between 41 and 55.

Stem	Leaf
2	2
3	4
4	1 4 7 8
5	1 5 5

$4|1 = 41$

Chapter 2   27   Course 1

2-4 Lesson Reading Guide

NAME _____ DATE _____ PERIOD _____

Stem-and-Leaf Plots

Get Ready for the Lesson

Complete the activity at the top of page 92 in your textbook. Write your answers below.

1. What were the least and greatest number of instant messages sent? **2; 45**

2. Which number of instant messages occurred most often? **21**

Read the Lesson

3. In a stem-and-leaf plot, in what order are the data? **from least to greatest**

4. In a stem-and-leaf plot of two-digit numbers, how are the data represented? **The tens digits form the stems. The ones digits form the leaves.**

5. Look at the stem-and-leaf plot at the top of page 93. Of the twenty tallest waterfalls, how many are between 600 and 699 feet tall? Using the stem-and-leaf plot, how can you tell that this height-range is most common? **5; Because there are more waterfalls between 600 and 699 than any other row in the stem-and-leaf plot.**

Remember What You Learned

6. Write the steps for making a stem-and-leaf plot. Show someone what a stem-and-leaf plot is, how to read one, and how to make one. **See students' work; Sample answer: 1) Order the data from least to greatest. 2) Draw a vertical line and write the stems to the left of the line in order from least to greatest. 3) Record the leaves for each stem, left to right from least to greatest. 4) Write a key that explains the stems and leaves.**

Chapter 2   26   Course 1

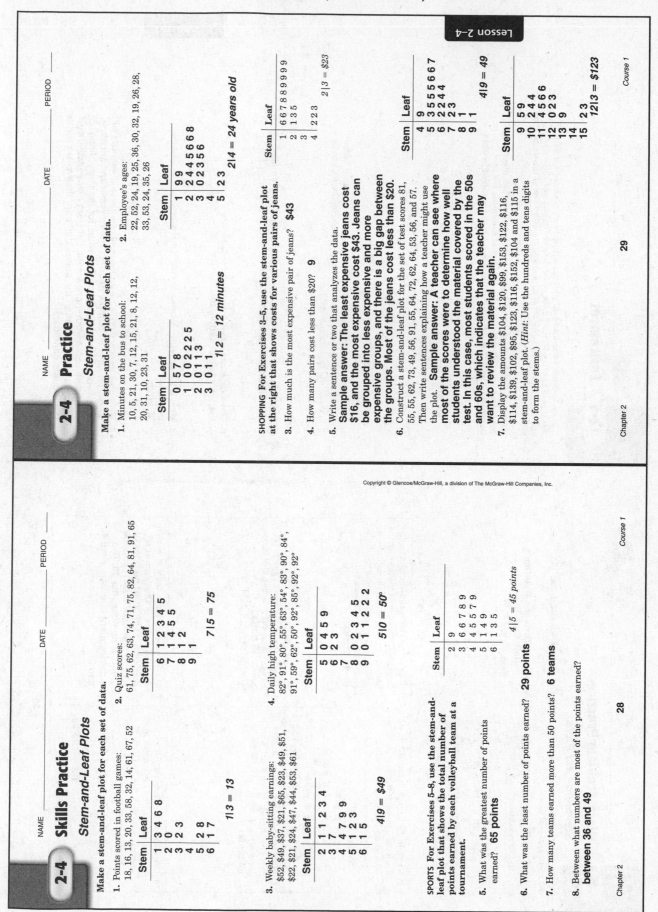

2-4 Skills Practice

Stem-and-Leaf Plots

NAME _____ DATE _____ PERIOD _____

Make a stem-and-leaf plot for each set of data.

1. Points scored in football games:
18, 16, 13, 20, 33, 58, 32, 14, 61, 67, 52

Stem	Leaf
1	3 4 6 8
2	0
3	2 3
4	
5	2 8
6	1 7

1|3 = 13

2. Quiz scores:
61, 75, 62, 63, 74, 71, 75, 82, 64, 81, 91, 65

Stem	Leaf
6	1 2 3 4 5
7	1 4 5 5
8	1 2
9	1

7|5 = 75

3. Weekly baby-sitting earnings:
$52, $49, $37, $21, $65, $23, $49, $51, $22, $21, $24, $47, $44, $53, $61

Stem	Leaf
2	1 1 2 3 4
3	7
4	4 7 9 9
5	1 2 3
6	1 5

4|9 = $49

4. Daily high temperature:
82°, 91°, 80°, 55°, 63°, 54°, 83°, 90°, 84°, 91°, 59°, 62°, 50°, 92°, 85°, 92°, 92°

Stem	Leaf
5	0 4 5 9
6	2 3
7	
8	0 2 3 4 5
9	0 1 1 2 2 2

5|0 = 50°

SPORTS For Exercises 5–8, use the stem-and-leaf plot that shows the total number of points earned by each volleyball team at a tournament.

Stem	Leaf
2	9
3	6 6 7 8 9
4	4 5 5 7 9
5	1 4 9
6	1 3 5

4|5 = 45 points

5. What was the greatest number of points earned? **65 points**

6. What was the least number of points earned? **29 points**

7. How many teams earned more than 50 points? **6 teams**

8. Between what numbers are most of the points earned? **between 36 and 49**

2-4 Practice

Stem-and-Leaf Plots

NAME _____ DATE _____ PERIOD _____

Make a stem-and-leaf plot for each set of data.

1. Minutes on the bus to school:
10, 5, 21, 30, 7, 12, 15, 21, 8, 12, 12, 20, 31, 10, 23, 31

Stem	Leaf
0	5 7 8
1	0 0 2 2 2 5
2	0 1 1 3
3	0 1 1

1|2 = 12 minutes

2. Employee's ages:
22, 52, 24, 19, 25, 36, 30, 32, 19, 26, 28, 33, 53, 24, 35, 26

Stem	Leaf
1	9 9
2	2 4 4 5 6 6 8
3	0 2 3 5 6
4	
5	2 3

2|4 = 24 years old

SHOPPING For Exercises 3–5, use the stem-and-leaf plot at the right that shows costs for various pairs of jeans.

Stem	Leaf
1	6 6 7 8 9 9 9 9
2	1 3 5
3	
4	2 2 3

2|3 = $23

3. How much is the most expensive pair of jeans? **$43**

4. How many pairs cost less than $20? **9**

5. Write a sentence or two that analyzes the data. **Sample answer: The least expensive jeans cost $16, and the most expensive cost $43. Jeans can be grouped into less expensive and more expensive groups, and there is a big gap between the groups. Most of the jeans cost less than $20.**

6. Construct a stem-and-leaf plot for the set of test scores 81, 55, 55, 62, 73, 49, 56, 91, 55, 64, 72, 62, 64, 53, 56, and 57. Then write sentences explaining how a teacher might use the plot. **Sample answer: A teacher can see where most of the scores were to determine how well students understood the material covered by the test. In this case, most students scored in the 50s and 60s, which indicates that the teacher may want to review the material again.**

Stem	Leaf
4	9
5	3 5 5 5 6 6 7
6	2 2 4 4
7	2 3
8	1
9	1

4|9 = 49

7. Display the amounts $104, $120, $99, $153, $122, $116, $139, $102, $95, $123, $116, $152, $104 and $115 in a stem-and-leaf plot. (*Hint:* Use the hundreds and tens digits to form the stems.)

Stem	Leaf
9	5 9
10	2 4 4
11	4 5 6 6
12	0 2 3
13	9
14	
15	2 3

12|3 = $123

Answers

Answers (Lesson 2-4)

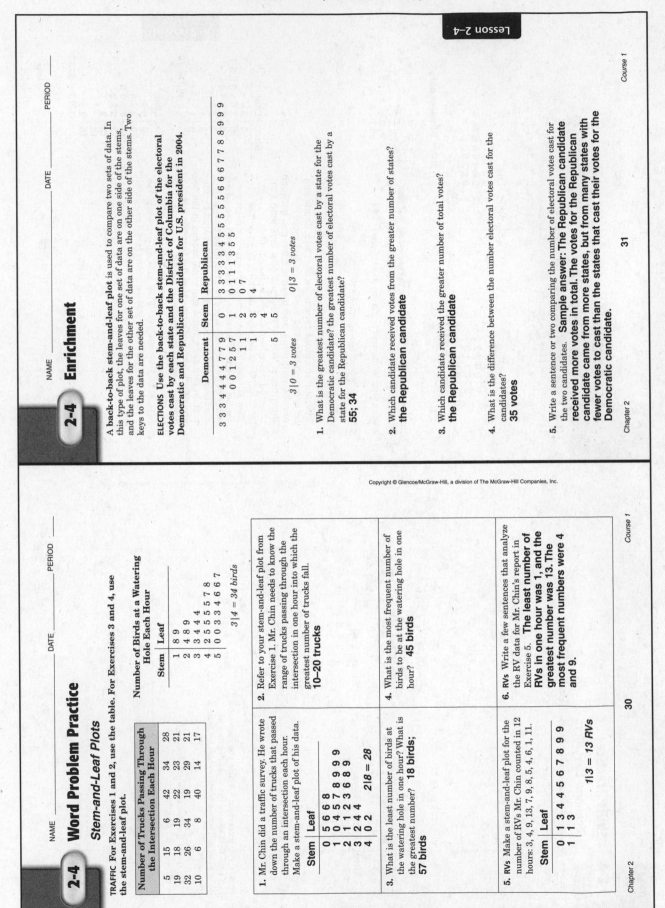

2-4 Word Problem Practice

Stem-and-Leaf Plots

TRAFFIC For Exercises 1 and 2, use the table. For Exercises 3 and 4, use the stem-and-leaf plot.

Number of Trucks Passing Through the Intersection Each Hour

5	15	6	42	34	28
19	18	19	22	23	21
32	26	34	19	29	21
10	6	8	40	14	17

1. Mr. Chin did a traffic survey. He wrote down the number of trucks that passed through an intersection each hour. Make a stem-and-leaf plot of his data.

Stem	Leaf
0	5 6 6 8
1	0 4 5 7 8 9 9 9
2	1 1 2 3 6 8 9
3	2 4 4
4	0 2

2|8 = 28

2. Refer to your stem-and-leaf plot from Exercise 1. Mr. Chin needs to know the range of trucks passing through the intersection in one hour into which the greatest number of trucks fall.
10–20 trucks

3. What is the least number of birds at the watering hole in one hour? What is the greatest number? **18 birds; 57 birds**

4. What is the most frequent number of birds to be at the watering hole in one hour? **45 birds**

5. **RVs** Make a stem-and-leaf plot for the number of RVs Mr. Chin counted in 12 hours: 3, 4, 9, 13, 7, 9, 8, 5, 4, 6, 1, 11.

Stem	Leaf
0	1 3 4 4 5 6 7 8 9 9
1	1 3

1|3 = 13 RVs

6. **RVs** Write a few sentences that analyze the RV data for Mr. Chin's report in Exercise 5. **The least number of RVs in one hour was 1, and the greatest number was 13. The most frequent numbers were 4 and 9.**

2-4 Enrichment

A **back-to-back stem-and-leaf plot** is used to compare two sets of data. In this type of plot, the leaves for one set of data are on one side of the stems, and the leaves for the other set of data are on the other side of the stems. Two keys to the data are needed.

ELECTIONS Use the back-to-back stem-and-leaf plot of the electoral votes cast by each state and the District of Columbia for the Democratic and Republican candidates for U.S. president in 2004.

Democrat	Stem	Republican
3 3 3 4 4 4 4 7 7 9	0	3 3 3 3 3 4 5 5 5 5 6 6 6 7 7 8 8 9 9 9
0 0 1 2 5 7	1	0 1 1 1 3 5 5
1 1	2	0 7
1	3	4
5	4	
5	5	

3|0 = 3 votes   0|3 = 3 votes

1. What is the greatest number of electoral votes cast by a state for the Democratic candidate? the greatest number of electoral votes cast by a state for the Republican candidate?
55; 34

2. Which candidate received votes from the greater number of states?
the Republican candidate

3. Which candidate received the greater number of total votes?
the Republican candidate

4. What is the difference between the number electoral votes cast for the candidates?
35 votes

5. Write a sentence or two comparing the number of electoral votes cast for the two candidates. **Sample answer: The Republican candidate received more votes in total. The votes for the Republican candidate came from more states, but from many states with fewer votes to cast than the states that cast their votes for the Democratic candidate.**

NAME _____ DATE _____ PERIOD _____

2-5 Study Guide and Intervention

Line Plots

A **line plot** is a diagram that shows the frequency of data on a number line. A line plot is created by drawing a number line and then placing an ✕ above a data value each time that data occurs.

Example 1 Make a line plot of the data in the table at the right.

Time Spent Traveling to School (minutes)					
5	6	3	10	12	15	5
10	5	8	12	5	5	8

Draw a number line. The smallest value is 3 minutes and the largest value is 15 minutes. So, you can use a scale of 0 to 15.

Put an ✕ above the number that represents the travel time of each student in the table. Be sure to include a title.

Example 2 How many students spend 5 minutes traveling to school each day?

Locate 5 on the number line and count the number of ✕'s above it. There are 5 students that travel 5 minutes to school each day.

Exercises

AGES For Exercises 1–3, use the data below.

Ages of Lifeguards at Brookville Swim Club				
16	16	20	22	18
18	17	18	25	17	19

1. Make a line plot of the data.

Ages of Lifeguards at Brookville Swim Club

2. How many of the lifeguards are 18 years old? **4**

3. What is the age difference between the oldest and youngest lifeguard at Brookville Swim Club? **9 years**

Chapter 2 33 Course 1

NAME _____ DATE _____ PERIOD _____

2-5 Lesson Reading Guide

Line Plots

Get Ready for the Lesson

Read the introduction at the top of page 96 in your textbook. Write your answers below.

1. How many of the animals have a life expectancy of 15 years? **2**

2. How many animals have a life expectancy from 5 to 10 years, including 10? **5**

3. What is the longest life expectancy represented? **20 yr**

4. What is the shortest life expectancy represented? **3 yr**

Read the Lesson

5. How is a line plot similar to plotting points on a number line? **Sample answer: You first locate the number on the number line. Then, instead of marking a point on the number line, you place an ✕ above the point.**

6. Describe one benefit of plotting data on a line plot. **Sample answer: You can easily identify the item that has the most values in a set of data.**

7. Explain how you can use a line plot to find out how spread out a group of data are. **Sample answer: You can find the least and greatest number on the line plot and then find their difference.**

Remember What You Learned

8. Work with a partner. Find a set of data from a survey, newspaper, or the Internet that can be used in a line plot. Create a line plot of the data along with two questions about the data. Switch your line plot and questions with another group. Use the line plots to answer the questions about the data. **See students' work.**

Chapter 2 32 Course 1

Answers (Lesson 2-5)

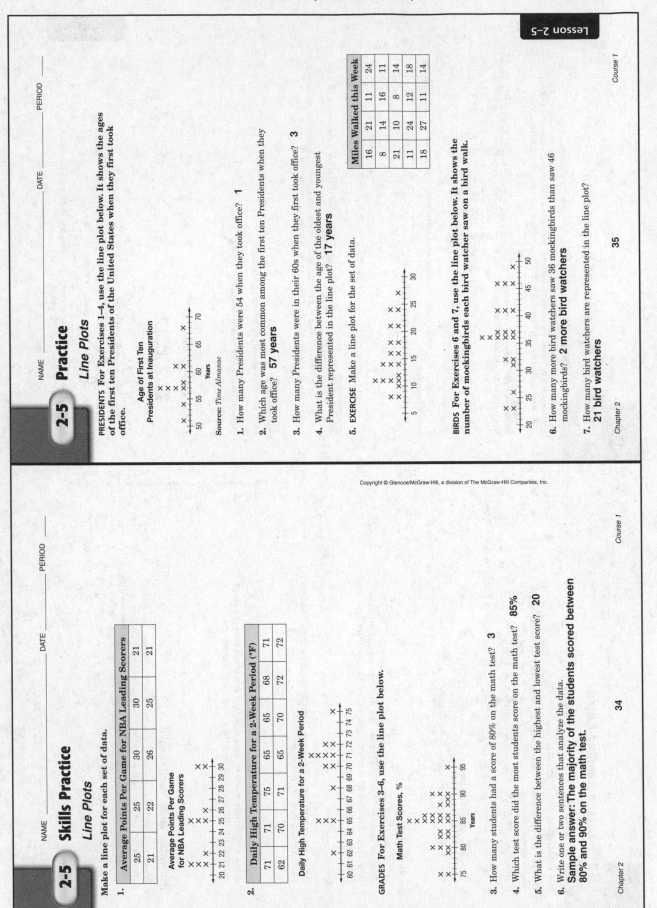

NAME _____ **DATE** _____ **PERIOD** _____

2-5 Practice

Line Plots

PRESIDENTS For Exercises 1–4, use the line plot below. It shows the ages of the first ten Presidents of the United States when they first took office.

Age of First Ten Presidents at Inauguration

(line plot)

Years   50   55   60   65   70

Source: *Time Almanac*

1. How many Presidents were 54 when they took office? **1**

2. Which age was most common among the first ten Presidents when they took office? **57 years**

3. How many Presidents were in their 60s when they first took office? **3**

4. What is the difference between the age of the oldest and youngest President represented in the line plot? **17 years**

5. **EXERCISE** Make a line plot for the set of data.

Miles Walked this Week					
16	21	11	24		
8	14	16	11		
21	10	8	14		
11	24	12	18		
18	27	11	14		

(line plot)

5   10   15   20   25   30

BIRDS For Exercises 6 and 7, use the line plot below. It shows the number of mockingbirds each bird watcher saw on a bird walk.

(line plot)

20   25   30   35   40   45   50

6. How many more bird watchers saw 36 mockingbirds than saw 46 mockingbirds? **2 more bird watchers**

7. How many bird watchers are represented in the line plot? **21 bird watchers**

Chapter 2   35   *Course 1*

NAME _____ **DATE** _____ **PERIOD** _____

2-5 Skills Practice

Line Plots

Make a line plot for each set of data.

1.

Average Points Per Game for NBA Leading Scorers			
25	25	30	21
21	22	26	21

Average Points Per Game for NBA Leading Scorers

(line plot)

20 21 22 23 24 25 26 27 28 29 30
Years

2.

Daily High Temperature for a 2-Week Period (°F)			
71	75	65	68	71
62	70	71	70	72

Daily High Temperature for a 2-Week Period

(line plot)

60 61 62 63 64 65 66 67 68 69 70 71 72 73 74 75

GRADES For Exercises 3–6, use the line plot below.

Math Test Scores, %

(line plot)

75   80   85   90   95
Years

3. How many students had a score of 80% on the math test? **3**

4. Which test score did the most students score on the math test? **85%**

5. What is the difference between the highest and lowest test score? **20**

6. Write one or two sentences that analyze the data.
Sample answer: The majority of the students scored between 80% and 90% on the math test.

Chapter 2   34   *Course 1*

Answers (Lesson 2-5)

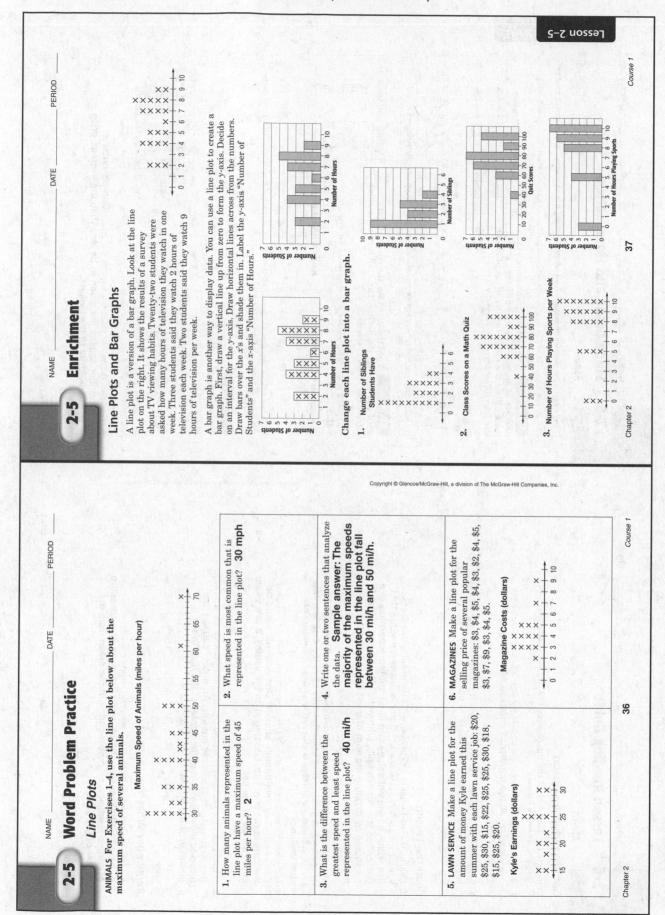

NAME _____ DATE _____ PERIOD _____

2-5 Word Problem Practice

Line Plots

ANIMALS For Exercises 1–4, use the line plot below about the maximum speed of several animals.

Maximum Speed of Animals (miles per hour)

1. How many animals represented in the line plot have a maximum speed of 45 miles per hour? **2**

2. What speed is most common that is represented in the line plot? **30 mph**

3. What is the difference between the greatest speed and least speed represented in the line plot? **40 mi/h**

4. Write one or two sentences that analyze the data. **Sample answer: The majority of the maximum speeds represented in the line plot fall between 30 mi/h and 50 mi/h.**

5. **LAWN SERVICE** Make a line plot for the amount of money Kyle earned this summer with each lawn service job: $20, $25, $30, $15, $22, $25, $30, $18, $15, $25, $20.

Kyle's Earnings (dollars)

6. **MAGAZINES** Make a line plot for the selling price of several popular magazines: $3, $4, $5, $4, $3, $2, $4, $5, $3, $7, $9, $3, $4, $5.

Magazine Costs (dollars)

Chapter 2   36   Course 1

NAME _____ DATE _____ PERIOD _____

2-5 Enrichment

Line Plots and Bar Graphs

A line plot is a version of a bar graph. Look at the line plot on the right. It shows the results of a survey about TV viewing habits. Twenty-two students were asked how many hours of television they watch in one week. Three students said they watch 2 hours of television each week. Two students said they watch 9 hours of television per week.

A bar graph is another way to display data. You can use a line plot to create a bar graph. First, draw a vertical line up from zero to form the y-axis. Decide on an interval for the y-axis. Draw horizontal lines across from the numbers. Draw bars over the x's and shade them in. Label the y-axis "Number of Students" and the x-axis "Number of Hours."

Change each line plot into a bar graph.

1. Number of Siblings Students Have

2. Class Scores on a Math Quiz

3. Number of Hours Playing Sports per Week

Chapter 2   37   Course 1

Chapter 2   **A15**   Course 1

NAME _____ DATE _____ PERIOD _____

2-6 Study Guide and Intervention

Mean

The **mean** is the most common measure of central tendency. It is an average, so it describes all of the data in a data set.

Example 1 The picture graph shows the number of members on four different swim teams. Find the mean number of members for the four different swim teams.

Swim Team Members	
Amberly	𝕏𝕏𝕏𝕏𝕏𝕏𝕏𝕏𝕏
Carlton	𝕏𝕏𝕏𝕏𝕏𝕏𝕏𝕏𝕏𝕏𝕏
Hamilton	𝕏𝕏𝕏𝕏𝕏𝕏
Westleigh	𝕏𝕏𝕏𝕏𝕏𝕏𝕏𝕏𝕏𝕏

Simplify an expression.

$$\text{mean} = \frac{9 + 11 + 6 + 10}{4}$$

$$= \frac{36}{4} \text{ or } 9$$

A set of data may contain very high or very low values. These values are called **outliers**.

Example 2 Find the mean for the snowfall data with and without the outlier. Then tell how the outlier affects the mean of the data.

Month	Snowfall (in.)
Nov.	20
Dec.	19
Jan.	20
Feb.	17
Mar.	4

Compared to the other values, 4 inches is low. So, it is an outlier.

mean with outlier

$$\text{mean} = \frac{20 + 19 + 20 + 17 + 4}{5}$$

$$= \frac{80}{5} \text{ or } 16$$

mean without outlier

$$\text{mean} = \frac{20 + 19 + 20 + 17}{4}$$

$$= \frac{76}{4} \text{ or } 19$$

With the outlier, the mean is less than the values of most of the data. Without the outlier, the mean is close in value to the data.

Exercises

SHOPPING For Exercises 1–3, use the bar graph at the right.

Jacket Prices

1. Find the mean of the data. **$21**

2. Which jacket price is an outlier? **$9**

3. Find the mean of the data if the outlier is not included. **$24**

4. How does the outlier affect the mean of the data? **Sample answer: The outlier causes the mean to be less than the average price of the jackets.**

NAME _____ DATE _____ PERIOD _____

2-6 Lesson Reading Guide

Mean

Get Ready for the Lesson

Complete the Mini Lab at the top of page 102 in your textbook. Write your answers below.

1. On average, how many inches did it snow per day in five days? Explain your reasoning. **3; the number of cubes in each stack is 3.**

2. Suppose on the sixth day it snowed 9 inches. If you moved the cubes again, how many cubes would be in each stack? **4 cubes**

Read the Lesson

3. Look up the word *mean* in a dictionary. Write the meaning that fits the way the word is used in this lesson. **Sample answer: a value that lies within a range of values and is computed according to a prescribed law; for example, arithmetic mean (a value that is computed by dividing the sum of a set of terms by the number of terms)**

Look at the paragraph below the activity at the top of page 102 in your textbook. A number that helps describe all of the data in a data set is an average. An average is also referred to as a measure of central tendency.

4. Is the mean a good measure of central tendency when there is no outlier? Give an example. **Yes; Sample answer: One example could be the data in the Mini Lab. Looking at all the values, 3 is a value in the center of the set.**

5. Is the mean a good measure of central tendency when there is an outlier? Give an example. **No; Sample answer: An outlier causes the mean to move away from the center of the data in the direction of the outlier.**

Remember What You Learned

6. Explain one problem with using the mean as a measure of central tendency. **Sample answer: When using the mean as a measure of central tendency, an outlier can shift the mean from the center of the data.**

Answers (Lesson 2-6)

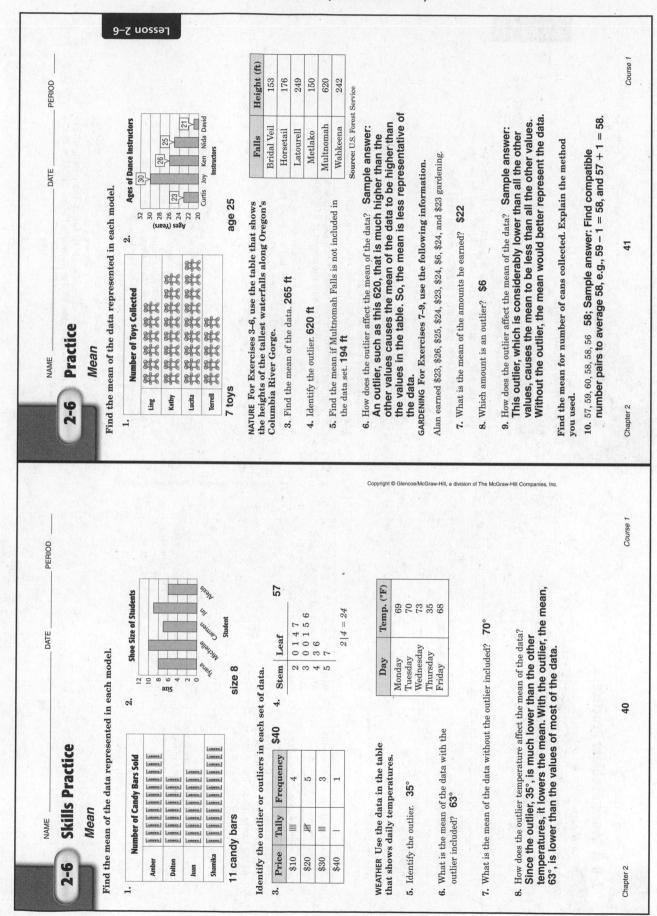

Lesson 2-6

NAME _____ DATE _____ PERIOD _____

2-6 Practice

Mean

Find the mean of the data represented in each model.

1.

Number of Toys Collected

Ling	🎀🎀🎀🎀🎀🎀
Kathy	🎀🎀🎀🎀🎀
Lucita	🎀🎀🎀🎀🎀🎀
Terrell	🎀🎀🎀🎀

7 toys

2.

Ages of Dance Instructors

age 25

NATURE For Exercises 3–6, use the table that shows the heights of the tallest waterfalls along Oregon's Columbia River Gorge.

Falls	Height (ft)
Bridal Veil	153
Horsetail	176
Latourell	249
Metlako	150
Multnomah	620
Wahkeena	242

Source: U.S. Forest Service

3. Find the mean of the data. **265 ft**

4. Identify the outlier. **620 ft**

5. Find the mean if Multnomah Falls is not included in the data set. **194 ft**

6. How does the outlier affect the mean of the data? **Sample answer: An outlier, such as this 620, that is much higher than the other values causes the mean of the data to be higher than the values in the table. So, the mean is less representative of the data.**

GARDENING For Exercises 7–9, use the following information.
Alan earned $23, $26, $25, $24, $23, $24, $6, $24, and $23 gardening.

7. What is the mean of the amounts he earned? **$22**

8. Which amount is an outlier? **$6**

9. How does the outlier affect the mean of the data? **Sample answer: This outlier, which is considerably lower than all the other values, causes the mean to be less than all the other values. Without the outlier, the mean would better represent the data.**

Find the mean for number of cans collected. Explain the method you used.

10. 57, 59, 60, 58, 58, 56   **58; Sample answer: Find compatible number pairs to average 58, e.g., 59 − 1 = 58, and 57 + 1 = 58.**

Chapter 2   41   *Course 1*

NAME _____ DATE _____ PERIOD _____

2-6 Skills Practice

Mean

Find the mean of the data represented in each model.

1.

Number of Candy Bars Sold

Amber	CANDY ×6
Dalton	CANDY ×13
Juan	CANDY ×13
Shamika	CANDY ×4

11 candy bars

2.

Shoe Size of Students

size 8

Identify the outlier or outliers in each set of data.

3.

Price	Tally	Frequency
$10	llll	4
$20	llll l	5
$30	lll	3
$40	l	1

$40

4.

Stem	Leaf
2	0 1 4 7
3	0 0 1 5 6
4	3 6
5	7

2 | 4 = 24   **57**

WEATHER Use the data in the table that shows daily temperatures.

Day	Temp. (°F)
Monday	69
Tuesday	70
Wednesday	73
Thursday	35
Friday	68

5. Identify the outlier. **35°**

6. What is the mean of the data with the outlier included? **63°**

7. What is the mean of the data without the outlier included? **70°**

8. How does the outlier temperature affect the mean of the data? **Since the outlier, 35°, is much lower than the other temperatures, it lowers the mean. With the outlier, the mean, 63°, is lower than the values of most of the data.**

Chapter 2   40   *Course 1*

Answers

Chapter 2   **A17**   *Course 1*

Answers (Lesson 2-6)

Word Problem Practice (2-6)

Mean

ANIMALS For Exercises 1–3, use the table about bears.

Bear	Average Height (ft)	Average Weight (lb)
Alaskan Brown	8	1,500
Black	6	338
Grizzly	7	588
Polar	7	850

1. You are writing a report on bears. You are analyzing the data on heights and weights in the table above. First look for outliers. Identify the outlier for the height data. Identify the outlier for the weight data. **none; 1,500 lb**

2. Find the mean of the bear weight data with and without the outlier. **819 lb; 592 lb**

3. Describe how the outlier affects the mean of the bear weight data. **Sample answer: Such an extremely high outlier causes the mean of the data to be considerably higher than the average weight of the majority of the bears. Thus, the mean is not representative of the data.**

4. **WORK** Carlos earned $23, $29, $25, $16, and $17 working at an ice cream shop after school. What is the mean amount he earned? **$22**

5. **CARS** The cost of a tank of gas at nine different gas stations is shown below. What was the mean cost of a tank of gas? **$19**
Cost of Gas: $17, $18, $22, $15, $17, $16, $25, $21, and $20

6. **SCHOOL** Sally received scores on math quizzes as shown below. Find her mean score with and without both outliers. **80; 89**
Quiz Scores: 84, 85, 91, 81, 52, 92, 99, 91, and 45

Enrichment (2-6)

Mean, Median, or Mode?

When most people hear the word "average," they think about what mathematicians call arithmetic mean. But the three measures of central tendency, mean, median and mode, are all different types of averages. Average is not a mathematical word. In mathematics, it is necessary to specify which type of average you are using.

1. The prices of seven homes for sale in Sunnydale are $151,000; $148,500; $163,000; $180,500; $151,000; $172,000; $189,000. Find the mean, median, and mode for the price of the homes for sale.
mean: $165,000; median: $163,000, mode: $151,000

2. A real estate agent is writing an advertisement for a newspaper. She writes, "The average price of a home in Sunnydale is $151,000." Which average did she use? Explain why she chose to use this particular average. Is this average misleading?
She used the mode. The reason she used this is because it is significantly lower than the median and the mean. It makes the homes in Sunnydale look inexpensive and more buyers will probably come to look at them.

3. Which type of average should be used to best represent the "average" price of a home in Sunnydale?
Either the median or the mean, because they are very similar. The median is $163,000 and the mean is $165,000.

A candy company is having a special promotion for which it includes special blue colored candies in its packages. The line plot shows how many blue candies were found in each of 19 packages.

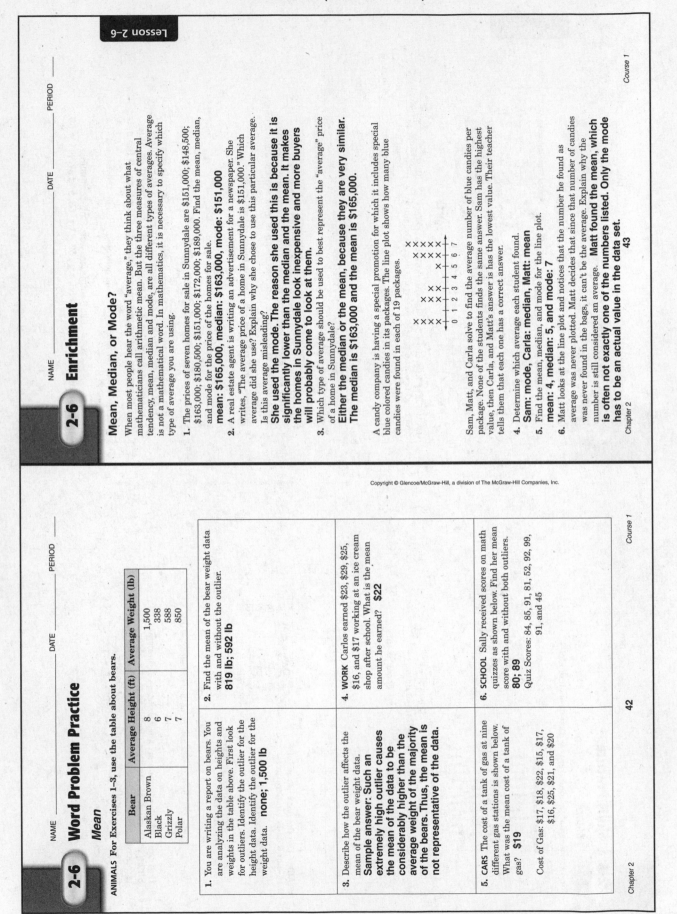

```
              x
          x   x
          x   x   x
      x   x   x   x
  x   x   x   x   x   x
  +---+---+---+---+---+---+---+
  0   1   2   3   4   5   6   7
```

Sam, Matt, and Carla solve to find the average number of blue candies per package. None of the students finds the same answer. Sam has the highest value, then Carla, and Matt's answer has the lowest value. Their teacher tells them that each one has a correct answer.

4. Determine which average each student found.
Sam: mode, Carla: median, Matt: mean

5. Find the mean, median, and mode for the line plot.
mean: 4, median: 5, and mode: 7

6. Matt looks at the line plot and notices that the number he found as average was never plotted. Matt decides that since that number of candies was never found in the bags, it can't be the average. Explain why the number is still considered an average. **Matt found the mean, which is often not exactly one of the numbers listed. Only the mode has to be an actual value in the data set.**

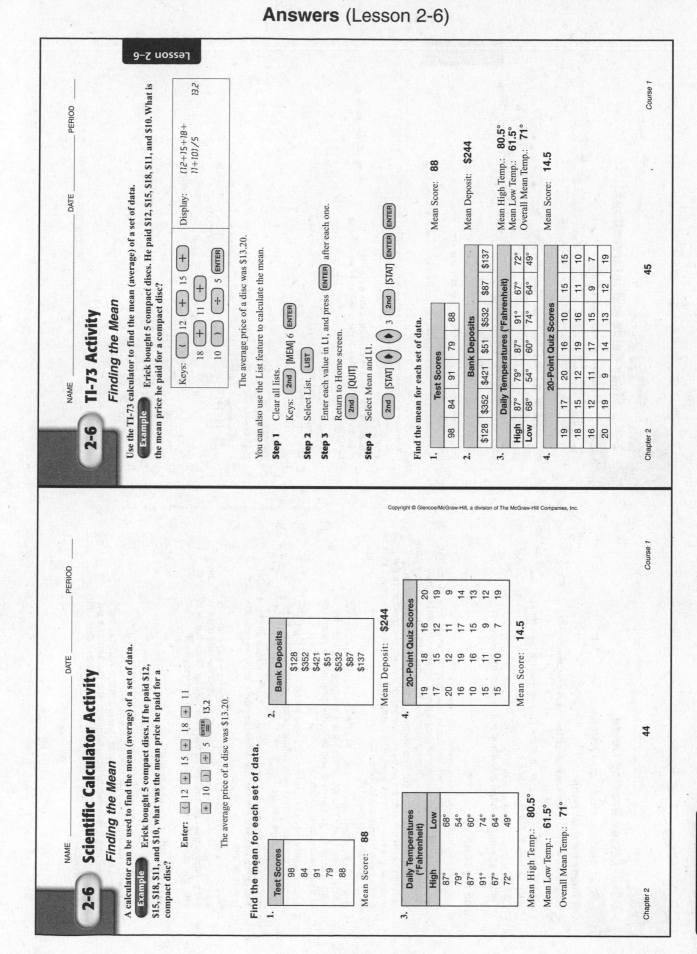

NAME _____ DATE _____ PERIOD _____

2-6 Scientific Calculator Activity

Finding the Mean

A calculator can be used to find the mean (average) of a set of data.

Example Erick bought 5 compact discs. If he paid $12, $15, $18, $11, and $10, what was the mean price he paid for a compact disc?

Enter: 12 [+] 15 [+] 18 [+] 11
[+] 10 [)] [÷] 5 [ENTER] 13.2

The average price of a disc was $13.20.

Find the mean for each set of data.

1.

Test Scores
98
84
91
79
88

Mean Score: **88**

2.

Bank Deposits
$128
$352
$421
$51
$532
$87
$137

Mean Deposit: **$244**

3.

Daily Temperatures (°Fahrenheit)	
High	**Low**
87°	68°
79°	54°
87°	60°
91°	74°
67°	64°
72°	49°

Mean High Temp.: **80.5°**
Mean Low Temp.: **61.5°**
Overall Mean Temp.: **71°**

4.

20-Point Quiz Scores				
19	18	16	16	20
17	15	12	11	19
20	12	11	17	9
16	19	17	15	14
10	16	15	9	13
15	11	9	12	
15	10	7	19	

Mean Score: **14.5**

NAME _____ DATE _____ PERIOD _____

2-6 TI-73 Activity

Finding the Mean

Use the TI-73 calculator to find the mean (average) of a set of data.

Example Erick bought 5 compact discs. He paid $12, $15, $18, $11, and $10. What is the mean price he paid for a compact disc?

Keys: [(] 12 [+] 15 [+]
18 [+] 11 [+]
10 [)] [÷] 5 [ENTER]

Display: (12+15+18+
11+10)/5
13.2

The average price of a disc was $13.20.

You can also use the List feature to calculate the mean.

Step 1 Clear all lists.
Keys: [2nd] [MEM] 6 [ENTER]

Step 2 Select List. [LIST]

Step 3 Enter each value in L1, and press [ENTER] after each one.
Return to Home screen.
[2nd] [QUIT]

Step 4 Select Mean and L1.
[2nd] [STAT] [▲] [▲] 3 [2nd] [STAT] [ENTER] [ENTER]

Find the mean for each set of data.

1.

Test Scores		
98	84	91	79	88

Mean Score: **88**

2.

Bank Deposits				
$128	$352	$421	$51	$532	$87	$137

Mean Deposit: **$244**

3.

Daily Temperatures (°Fahrenheit)					
High	87°	79°	87°	91°	67°	72°
Low	68°	54°	60°	74°	64°	49°

Mean High Temp.: **80.5°**
Mean Low Temp.: **61.5°**
Overall Mean Temp.: **71°**

4.

20-Point Quiz Scores				
19	17	20	16	10	15	15
18	15	12	19	16	11	10
16	12	11	17	15	9	7
20	19	9	14	13	12	19

Mean Score: **14.5**

Lesson 2-6

Answers

Lesson 2-7

2-7 Study Guide and Intervention
Median, Mode, and Range

The **median** is the middle number of the data put in order, or the mean of the middle two numbers.
The **mode** is the number or numbers that occur most often.

Example 1 The table shows the costs of seven different books. Find the mean, median, and mode of the data.

Book Costs ($)			
22	13	11	16
14	13	16	

mean: $\dfrac{22 + 13 + 11 + 16 + 14 + 13 + 16}{7} = \dfrac{105}{7}$ or 15

To find the median, write the data in order from least to greatest.
median: 11, 13, 13, ⑭ 16, 16, 22

To find the mode, find the number or numbers that occur most often.
mode: 11, ⑬⑬ 14, ⑯⑯ 22
The mean is $15. The median is $14. There are two modes, $13 and $16.

Whereas the measures of central tendency describe the average of a set of data, the **range** of a set of data describes how the data vary.

Example 2 Find the range of the data in the stem-and-leaf plot. Then write a sentence describing how the data vary.

Stem	Leaf
3	2
4	0
5	0 5
6	0 3

$3|2 = 32$

The greatest value is 63. The least value is 32. So, the range is $63 - 32$ or 31°. The range is large. It tells us that the data vary greatly in value.

Exercises

Find the mean, median, mode, and range of each set of data.

1. hours worked: 14, 13, 14, 16, 8
13; 14; 14; 8

2. points scored by football team: 29, 31, 14, 21, 31, 22, 20
24; 22; 31; 17

3. [bar graph: Quiz Scores — Score vs. Abigail 72, Brian 60, Leisha 80, Marcus 68, Ryan 72, Takara 86]
73; 72; 72; 26

4. [line plot: Snowfall (inches), 0–10]
4; 3; 3; 8

Chapter 2 — 47 — Course 1

2-7 Lesson Reading Guide
Median, Mode, and Range

Get Ready for the Lesson

Complete the activity at the top of page 108 in your textbook. Write your answers below.

1. Order the data from least to greatest. Which piece of data is in the middle of this list? **4, 5, 7, 8, 9, 9, 15; 8**

2. Compare this number to the mean of the data.
Sample answer: Both the mean and the median are about 8.

Read the Lesson

3. How are mean, median, and mode similar? How are they different?
Sample answer: All three are similar in that they are measures of central tendency and indicate centers of data sets; they are different by their definitions. The mean is found by dividing the sum of all the values by the number of values in the set. The median is the middle number of an ordered set. If the set has an even number of values, the median is the mean of the two middle values. The mode is the number or numbers that occur most frequently in the set.

Look at Example 4 on page 110.

4. How would you find the average of the data? What is another term for the average of the data? **You would find the average of the data by adding together all the data and then dividing by the number of data values given; Mean.**

5. What is causing the mean to be so high? **The mean is very high because the two largest data values are so much higher than the smallest data values.**

6. If there were two deserts of 250,000 square miles, how would this affect the mean? **The mean would be lower since the new data value is less than the previous mean.**

7. Does this example illustrate the statement, "Some averages may describe a data set better than other averages"? **Yes. The mean for this data set is higher than all but one of the data values. Because of this, the mean does not describe the date set very well.**

Remember What You Learned

8. You may already know that a median strip refers to the concrete or landscaped divider that runs down the center of many roads. How does this idea of median relate to the meaning of median in this lesson? **Sample answer: A median strip is located in the middle of a road, dividing it into two halves. Similarly, the median of a set of data is the middle value, the value that divides the data into two halves.**

Chapter 2 — 46 — Course 1

Answers (Lesson 2-7)

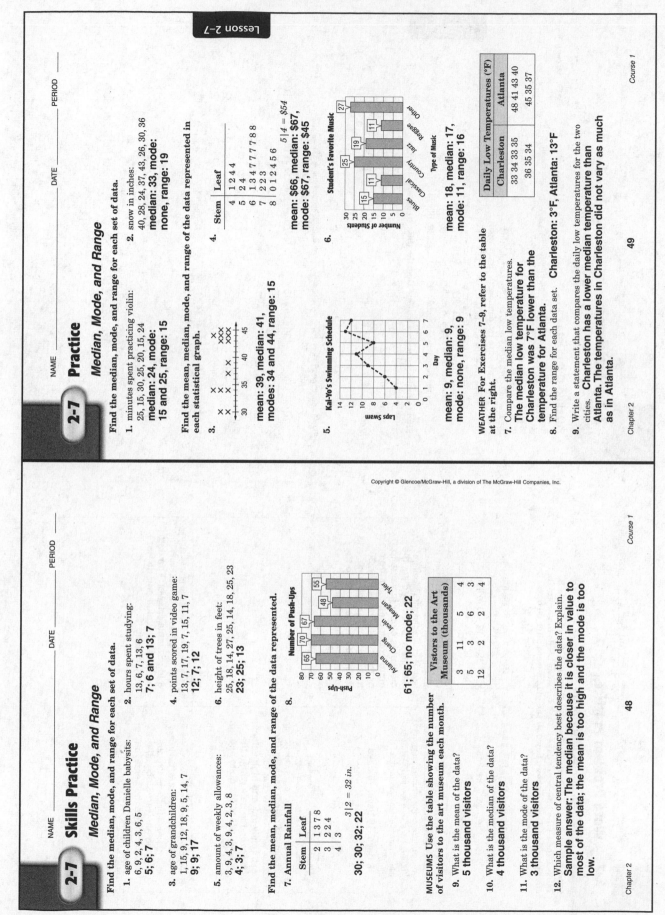

NAME _____ DATE _____ PERIOD _____

2-7 Skills Practice

Median, Mode, and Range

Find the median, mode, and range for each set of data.

1. age of children Danielle babysits:
6, 9, 2, 4, 3, 6, 5
5; 6; 7

2. hours spent studying:
13, 6, 7, 13, 6
7; 6 and 13; 7

3. age of grandchildren:
1, 15, 9, 12, 18, 9, 5, 14, 7
9; 9; 17

4. points scored in video game:
13, 7, 17, 19, 7, 15, 11, 7
12; 7; 12

5. amount of weekly allowances:
3, 9, 4, 3, 9, 4, 2, 3, 8
4; 3; 7

6. height of trees in feet:
25, 18, 14, 27, 25, 14, 18, 25, 23
23; 25; 13

Find the mean, median, mode, and range of the data represented.

7. Annual Rainfall

Stem	Leaf
2	1 3 7 8
3	2 2 4
4	3

3|2 = 32 in.

30; 30; 32; 22

8.

Number of Push-Ups

61; 65; no mode; 22

MUSEUMS Use the table showing the number of visitors to the art museum each month.

Visitors to the Art Museum (thousands)		
3	11	5	4
5	3	6	3
12	2	2	4

9. What is the mean of the data?
5 thousand visitors

10. What is the median of the data?
4 thousand visitors

11. What is the mode of the data?
3 thousand visitors

12. Which measure of central tendency best describes the data? Explain.
Sample answer: The median because it is closer in value to most of the data; the mean is too high and the mode is too low.

Chapter 2   48   *Course 1*

NAME _____ DATE _____ PERIOD _____

2-7 Practice

Median, Mode, and Range

Find the median, mode, and range for each set of data.

1. minutes spent practicing violin:
25, 15, 30, 25, 20, 15, 24
median: 24, mode: 15 and 25, range: 15

2. snow in inches:
40, 28, 24, 37, 43, 26, 30, 36
median: 33, mode: none, range: 19

Find the mean, median, mode, and range of the data represented in each statistical graph.

3.

mean: 39, median: 41, modes: 34 and 44, range: 15

4.

Stem	Leaf
4	1 2 4 4
5	2 4
6	1 3 4 7 7 7 7 8 8
7	2 2 3
8	0 1 2 4 5 6

5|4 = $54

mean: $66, median: $67, mode: $67, range: $45

5.

Kai-Yo's Swimming Schedule

mean: 9, median: 9, mode: none, range: 9

6.

Student's Favorite Music

mean: 18, median: 17, mode: 11, range: 16

WEATHER For Exercises 7–9, refer to the table at the right.

Daily Low Temperatures (°F)	
Charleston	**Atlanta**
33 34 33 35	48 41 43 40
36 35 34	45 35 37

7. Compare the median low temperature for Charleston and the temperature for Atlanta.
The median low temperature for Charleston was 7°F lower than the temperature for Atlanta.

8. Find the range for each data set.
Charleston: 3°F, Atlanta: 13°F

9. Write a statement that compares the daily low temperatures for the two cities.
Charleston has a lower median temperature than Atlanta. The temperatures in Charleston did not vary as much as in Atlanta.

Chapter 2   49   *Course 1*

Answers

Lesson 2-7

2-7 Enrichment

Puzzling Over Data

Each puzzle on this page contains an incomplete set of data. The clues give you information about the mean, median, mode, or range of the data. Working from these clues, you can decide what the missing data items must be. For example, this is how you might solve the data puzzle at the right.

Clue: mean = 18

Data: 12, 17, 18, 19, 19, ☐

There are 6 items of data.
The mean is 18, so the sum of the data must be 6 × 18 = 108.
Add the given data: 12 + 17 + 18 + 19 + 19 = 85.
Subtract from 108: 108 − 85 = 23.

So the complete set of data is: 12, 17, 18, 19, 19, 23.

Find the missing data. (Assume that the data items are listed in order from least to greatest.)

1. *Clue:* mode = 8

   Data: 7, 7, 8, **8**, **8**, 14

2. *Clue:* median = 54.5

   Data: 36, 40, 49, **60**, 65, 84

3. *Clues:* mean = 27
   mode = 30

   Data: 10, 25, 27, **30**, 30, **40**

4. *Clues:* median = 120
   range = 46

   Data: 110, 112, **116**, 124, 136, **156**

5. *Clues:* mean = 13
   median = 13
   range = 13

   Data: **6**, 9, 12, **14**, 18, **19**

6. *Clues:* mean = 7
   median = 8.5
   mode = 10

   Data: **1**, 4, 8, **9**, **10**, **10**

7. *Clues:* mean = 60
   mode = 52
   range = 28

   Data: **50**, 52, **52**, **56**, 72, 78

8. *Clues:* median = 24
   mode = 28
   range = 24

   Data: 6, 15, **20**, **28**, **28**, **30**

2-7 Word Problem Practice
Median, Mode, and Range

SCIENCE For Exercises 1–3, use Table A. For Exercises 4–6, use Table B. Table A shows the number of days it took for some seeds to germinate after planting. Table B shows how tall the plants were after 60 days.

Table A

Number of Days for Seeds to Germinate				
15	20	30	15	16
9	21	21	15	

Table B

Height (in.) of Plants After 60 Days				
17	19	13	17	20
15	17	21	14	

1. Refer to Table A. You are doing some experiments with germinating seeds. You are preparing a report on your findings to a seed company. What are the mean, median, and mode of the data?
18 days; 16 days; 15 days

2. Use your answer from Exercise 1. Which measure of central tendency best describes the data? Explain.
Sample answer: Median; the median is closer in value to more of the data than the mean or the mode. The outlier, 30, makes the mean too high, and the mode is too close to the lower end of the data.

3. What is the range of the seed germination data? Describe how the data vary.
21 days; Sample answer: The data vary widely due to extremely low and high values; however, the data within the middle values are quite similar.

4. What are the mean, median, and mode of the plant height data?
17 in.; 17 in.; 17 in.

5. Refer to your answer in Exercise 4. Which measure of central tendency best describes the data? Explain.
Sample answer: Since all the measures are the same, any of them describes the data well.

6. What is the range of the plant height data? Describe how the data vary.
8 in.; Sample answer: The data are close in value and do not vary greatly.

Answers (Lessons 2-7 and 2-8)

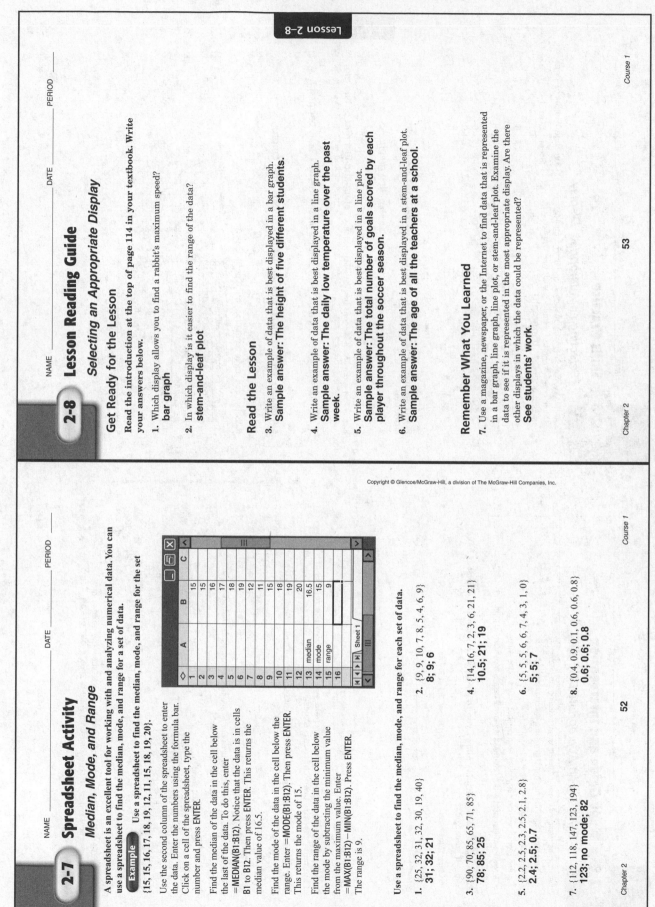

2-7

NAME _____ DATE _____ PERIOD _____

Spreadsheet Activity
Median, Mode, and Range

A spreadsheet is an excellent tool for working with and analyzing numerical data. You can use a spreadsheet to find the median, mode, and range for a set of data.

Example Use a spreadsheet to find the median, mode, and range for the set {15, 15, 16, 17, 18, 19, 12, 11, 15, 18, 19, 20}.

Use the second column of the spreadsheet to enter the data. Enter the numbers using the formula bar. Click on a cell of the spreadsheet, type the number and press ENTER.

Find the median of the data in the cell below the last of the data. To do this, enter =MEDIAN(B1:B12). Notice that the data is in cells B1 to B12. Then press ENTER. This returns the median value of 16.5.

Find the mode of the data in the cell below the range. Enter =MODE(B1:B12). Then press ENTER. This returns the mode of 15.

Find the range of the data in the cell below the mode by subtracting the minimum value from the maximum value. Enter =MAX(B1:B12)−MIN(B1:B12). Press ENTER. The range is 9.

◇	A	B	C
1		15	
2		15	
3		16	
4		17	
5		18	
6		19	
7		12	
8		11	
9		15	
10		18	
11		19	
12		20	
13	median	16.5	
14	mode	15	
15	range	9	
16			

Sheet 1

Use a spreadsheet to find the median, mode, and range for each set of data.

1. {25, 32, 31, 32, 30, 19, 40}
   31; 32; 21

2. {9, 9, 10, 7, 8, 5, 4, 6, 9}
   8; 9; 6

3. {90, 70, 85, 65, 71, 85}
   78; 85; 25

4. {14, 16, 7, 2, 3, 6, 21, 21}
   10.5; 21; 19

5. {2.2, 2.5, 2.3, 2.5, 2.1, 2.8}
   2.4; 2.5; 0.7

6. {5, 5, 5, 6, 6, 7, 4, 3, 1, 0}
   5; 5; 7

7. {112, 118, 147, 123, 194}
   123; no mode; 82

8. {0.4, 0.9, 0.1, 0.6, 0.6, 0.8}
   0.6; 0.6; 0.8

2-8

NAME _____ DATE _____ PERIOD _____

Lesson Reading Guide
Selecting an Appropriate Display

Get Ready for the Lesson

Read the introduction at the top of page 114 in your textbook. Write your answers below.

1. Which display allows you to find a rabbit's maximum speed?
   bar graph

2. In which display is it easier to find the range of the data?
   stem-and-leaf plot

Read the Lesson

3. Write an example of data that is best displayed in a bar graph.
   Sample answer: The height of five different students.

4. Write an example of data that is best displayed in a line graph.
   Sample answer: The daily low temperature over the past week.

5. Write an example of data that is best displayed in a line plot.
   Sample answer: The total number of goals scored by each player throughout the soccer season.

6. Write an example of data that is best displayed in a stem-and-leaf plot.
   Sample answer: The age of all the teachers at a school.

Remember What You Learned

7. Use a magazine, newspaper, or the Internet to find data that is represented in a bar graph, line graph, line plot, or stem-and-leaf plot. Examine the data to see if it is represented in the most appropriate display. Are there other displays in which the data could be represented?
   See students' work.

Answers

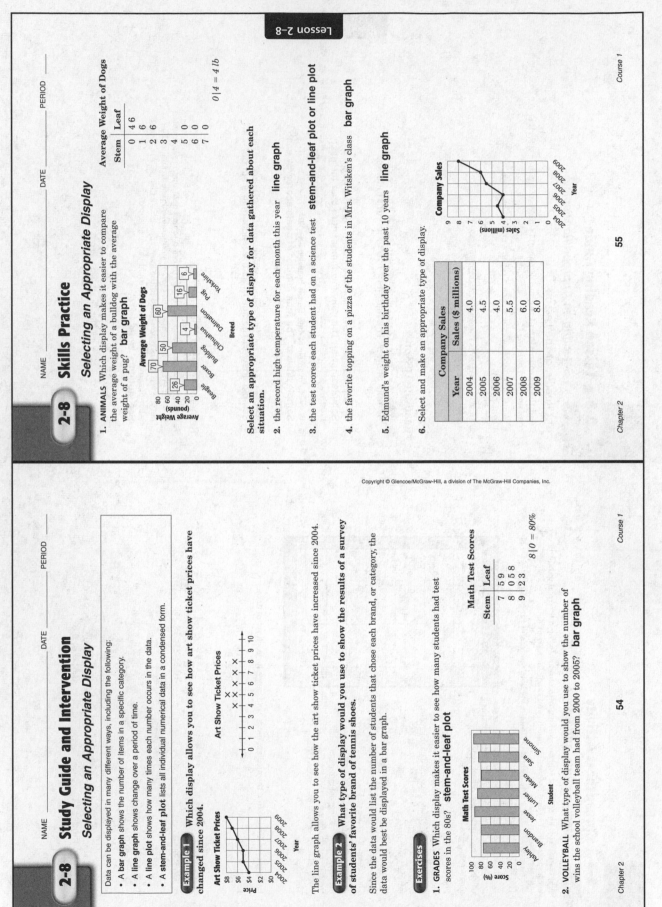

Lesson 2-8

2-8 Skills Practice

Selecting an Appropriate Display

NAME _____ DATE _____ PERIOD _____

1. ANIMALS Which display makes it easier to compare the average weight of a bulldog with the average weight of a pug? **bar graph**

Average Weight of Dogs (bar graph)

Average Weight of Dogs
Stem	Leaf
0	4 6
1	6
2	6
3	
4	
5	0
6	0 0
7	0

$0|4 = 4$ lb

Select an appropriate type of display for data gathered about each situation.

2. the record high temperature for each month this year **line graph**

3. the test scores each student had on a science test **stem-and-leaf plot or line plot**

4. the favorite topping on a pizza of the students in Mrs. Witsken's class **bar graph**

5. Edmund's weight on his birthday over the past 10 years **line graph**

6. Select and make an appropriate type of display.

Company Sales
Year	Sales ($ millions)
2004	4.0
2005	4.5
2006	4.0
2007	5.5
2008	6.0
2009	8.0

Company Sales (line graph)

Chapter 2   55   Course 1

2-8 Study Guide and Intervention

Selecting an Appropriate Display

NAME _____ DATE _____ PERIOD _____

Data can be displayed in many different ways, including the following:
- A **bar graph** shows the number of items in a specific category.
- A **line graph** shows change over a period of time.
- A **line plot** shows how many times each number occurs in the data.
- A **stem-and-leaf plot** lists all individual numerical data in a condensed form.

Example 1 Which display allows you to see how art show ticket prices have changed since 2004.

Art Show Ticket Prices (line graph)

Art Show Ticket Prices (line plot)

The line graph allows you to see how the art show ticket prices have increased since 2004.

Example 2 What type of display would you use to show the results of a survey of students' favorite brand of tennis shoes.

Since the data would list the number of students that chose each brand, or category, the data would best be displayed in a bar graph.

Exercises

1. GRADES Which display makes it easier to see how many students had test scores in the 80s? **stem-and-leaf plot**

Math Test Scores (bar graph)

Math Test Scores
Stem	Leaf
7	5 9
8	0 5 8
9	2 3

$8|0 = 80\%$

2. VOLLEYBALL What type of display would you use to show the number of wins the school volleyball team had from 2000 to 2005? **bar graph**

Chapter 2   54   Course 1

Answers (Lesson 2-8)

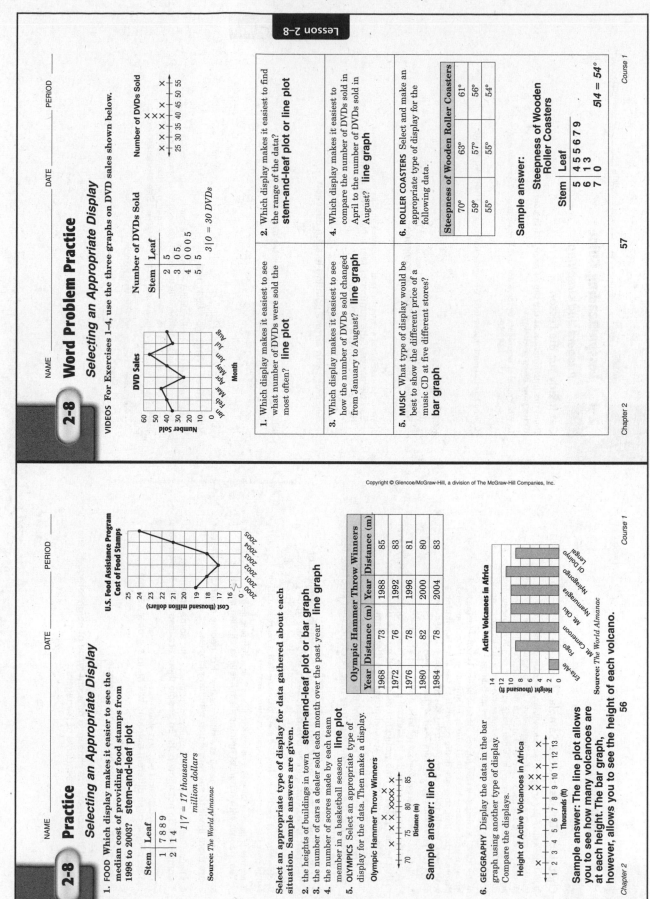

2-8 Word Problem Practice

NAME _____ DATE _____ PERIOD _____

Selecting an Appropriate Display

VIDEOS For Exercises 1–4, use the three graphs on DVD sales shown below.

DVD Sales

Number Sold — Month (Jan, Feb, Mar, Apr, May, Jun, Jul, Aug)

Number of DVDs Sold

Stem	Leaf
2	5
3	0 5
4	0 0 0 5
5	5

$3|0 = 30$ DVDs

Number of DVDs Sold (line plot): 25 30 35 40 45 50 55

1. Which display makes it easiest to see what number of DVDs were sold the most often? **line plot**

2. Which display makes it easiest to find the range of the data? **stem-and-leaf plot or line plot**

3. Which display makes it easiest to see how the number of DVDs sold changed from January to August? **line graph**

4. Which display makes it easiest to compare the number of DVDs sold in April to the number of DVDs sold in August? **line graph**

5. **MUSIC** What type of display would be best to show the different price of a music CD at five different stores? **bar graph**

6. **ROLLER COASTERS** Select and make an appropriate type of display for the following data.

Steepness of Wooden Roller Coasters

70°	63°	61°
59°	57°	56°
55°	55°	54°

Sample answer:

Steepness of Wooden Roller Coasters

Stem	Leaf
5	4 5 5 6 7 9
6	1 3
7	0

$5|4 = 54°$

Chapter 2   57   Course 1

2-8 Practice

NAME _____ DATE _____ PERIOD _____

Selecting an Appropriate Display

1. **FOOD** Which display makes it easier to see the median cost of providing food stamps from 1998 to 2003? **stem-and-leaf plot**

Stem	Leaf
1	7 8 8 9
2	1 4

$1|7 = 17$ thousand million dollars

Source: *The World Almanac*

U.S. Food Assistance Program Cost of Food Stamps

Cost (thousand million dollars): 16 17 18 19 20 21 22 23 24 25 — Year 2000 2001 2002 2003 2004 2005

Select an appropriate type of display for data gathered about each situation. Sample answers are given.

2. the heights of buildings in town **stem-and-leaf plot or bar graph**

3. the number of cars a dealer sold each month over the past year **line graph**

4. the number of scores made by each team member in a basketball season **line plot**

5. **OLYMPICS** Select an appropriate type of display for the data. Then make a display.

Olympic Hammer Throw Winners

Year	Distance (m)	Year	Distance (m)
1968	73	1988	85
1972	76	1992	83
1976	78	1996	81
1980	82	2000	80
1984	78	2004	83

Sample answer: line plot

Olympic Hammer Throw Winners

Distance (m): 70 75 80 85

6. **GEOGRAPHY** Display the data in the bar graph using another type of display. Compare the displays.

Active Volcanoes in Africa

Height (thousand ft): volcanoes — Erta-Ale, Fogo, Mt. Cameroon, Mt. Oku, Nyamuragira, Nyiragongo, Ol Donyo Lengai

Source: *The World Almanac*

Height of Active Volcanoes in Africa

Thousands (ft): 1 2 3 4 5 6 7 8 9 10 11 12 13

Sample answer: The line plot allows you to see how many volcanoes are at each height. The bar graph, however, allows you to see the height of each volcano.

Chapter 2   56   Course 1

Answers

Answers (Lessons 2-8 and 2-9)

2-9 Lesson Reading Guide

Integers and Graphing

NAME _____ DATE _____ PERIOD _____

Get Ready for the Lesson

Read the introduction at the top of page 121 in your textbook. Write your answers below.

1. What number represents owing 5 dollars? What number represents having 8 dollars left? **−$5, $8**

2. Who has the most money left? Who owes the most? **Thomas; Blake**

Read the Lesson

3. Write an example of a situation that a positive number could represent.
Sample answer: the height of someone

4. Write an example of a situation that a negative number could represent.
Sample answer: the number of feet a mountain climber descended down a mountain

5. In the number lines shown in this lesson, how is "continues without end" indicated? **with arrows pointing in each direction**

6. How do values change as you move from left to right on a number line? **They increase.**

Remember What You Learned

7. Antonyms are two words that have opposite meanings, such as *cold* and *hot*. Integers can be described by the antonyms *negative* or *positive* or as being *above zero* or *below zero*. Make a table of antonyms that describe situations involving negative and positive integers. **See students' work.**

Negative Integer	Positive Integer
loss	gain

Chapter 2　　　　　59　　　　　*Course 1*

2-8 Enrichment

NAME _____ DATE _____ PERIOD _____

Choosing a Representative Sample

Statisticians often use samples to represent larger groups. For example, television ratings are based on the opinions of a few people who are surveyed about a program. The people surveyed are just part of the whole group of people who watched the program. When using samples, people taking surveys must make sure that their samples are representative of the larger group in order to ensure that their conclusions are not misleading.

ADVERTISING A company that makes athletic shoes is considering hiring a professional basketball player to appear in its commercials. Before hiring him, they are doing research to see if he is popular with teens. Would they get good survey results from taking a survey about the basketball player from each of these surveys?

1. 200 teens at a basketball game of the basketball player's team
A survey at a game of the basketball player's team would probably favor that team's players. This would not be a good choice unless they were trying to choose between several players on that team.

2. 25 teens at a shopping mall
The teens at a mall would represent the segment of the population that spend time at the mall. However, they may not represent all of the teens in the United States.

3. 500 students at a number of different middle and high schools
This sample is large, and if the schools are chosen in a number of different areas, this survey would probably give very good results.

Decide whether each location is a good place to find a representative sample for the selected survey. Justify your answer.

4. number of hours of television watched in a month at a shopping mall
Yes; people with different opinions are likely to all visit a mall.

5. favorite kind of entertainment at a movie theater **No; people at a movie theater are more likely to say they enjoy watching movies.**

6. whether families own pets in an apartment complex **No; some apartment complexes do not allow pets, so people there are less likely to own pets.**

7. taste test of a soft drink at a grocery store
Yes; people of all different opinions will be in a grocery store.

8. favorite teacher in a school cafeteria
Yes; all students will be in a school cafeteria.

9. teenagers' favorite magazine at five different high schools
Yes; if the schools are chosen in different types of neighborhoods, the sample will be representative of teenagers.

Chapter 2　　　　　58　　　　　*Course 1*

Answers (Lesson 2-9)

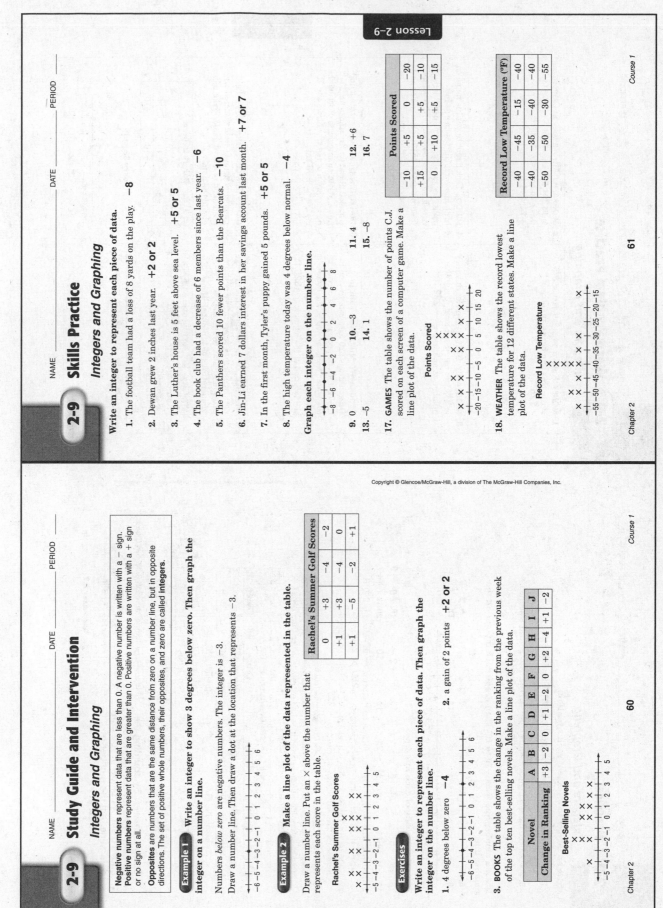

2-9 Skills Practice

NAME _____ DATE _____ PERIOD _____

Integers and Graphing

Write an integer to represent each piece of data.

1. The football team had a loss of 8 yards on the play. −8

2. Dewan grew 2 inches last year. +2 or 2

3. The Luther's house is 5 feet above sea level. +5 or 5

4. The book club had a decrease of 6 members since last year. −6

5. The Panthers scored 10 fewer points than the Bearcats. −10

6. Jin-Li earned 7 dollars interest in her savings account last month. +7 or 7

7. In the first month, Tyler's puppy gained 5 pounds. +5 or 5

8. The high temperature today was 4 degrees below normal. −4

Graph each integer on the number line.

9. 0   10. −3   11. 4   12. +6

13. −5   14. 1   15. −8   16. 7

−8 −6 −4 −2 0 2 4 6 8

17. **GAMES** The table shows the number of points C.J. scored on each screen of a computer game. Make a line plot of the data.

Points Scored		
−10	0	−20
+15	+5	−10
0	+10	−15

Points Scored

−20 −15 −10 −5 0 5 10 15 20

18. **WEATHER** The table shows the record lowest temperature for 12 different states. Make a line plot of the data.

Record Low Temperature (°F)		
−40	−45	−40
−40	−35	−40
−50	−50	−55

Record Low Temperature

−55 −50 −45 −40 −35 −30 −25 −20 −15

Chapter 2   61   *Course 1*

2-9 Study Guide and Intervention

NAME _____ DATE _____ PERIOD _____

Integers and Graphing

Negative numbers represent data that are less than 0. A negative number is written with a − sign.
Positive numbers represent data that are greater than 0. Positive numbers are written with a + sign or no sign at all.
Opposites are numbers that are the same distance from zero on a number line, but in opposite directions. The set of positive whole numbers, their opposites, and zero are called **integers**.

Example 1 Write an integer to show 3 degrees below zero. Then graph the integer on a number line.

Numbers *below zero* are negative numbers. The integer is −3.
Draw a number line. Then draw a dot at the location that represents −3.

−6 −5 −4 −3 −2 −1 0 1 2 3 4 5 6

Example 2 Make a line plot of the data represented in the table.

Draw a number line. Put an × above the number that represents each score in the table.

Rachel's Summer Golf Scores

0	−4	−4	−2
+1	+3	−4	0
+1	−5	−2	+1

Rachel's Summer Golf Scores

−5 −4 −3 −2 −1 0 1 2 3 4 5

Exercises

Write an integer to represent each piece of data. Then graph the integer on the number line.

1. 4 degrees below zero −4

−6 −5 −4 −3 −2 −1 0 1 2 3 4 5 6

2. a gain of 2 points +2 or 2

3. **BOOKS** The table shows the change in the ranking from the previous week of the top ten best-selling novels. Make a line plot of the data.

Novel	A	B	C	D	E	F	G	H	I	J
Change in Ranking	+3	−2	0	+1	−2	0	+2	−4	+1	−2

Best-Selling Novels

−5 −4 −3 −2 −1 0 1 2 3 4 5

Chapter 2   60   *Course 1*

Answers

Chapter 2   A27   *Course 1*

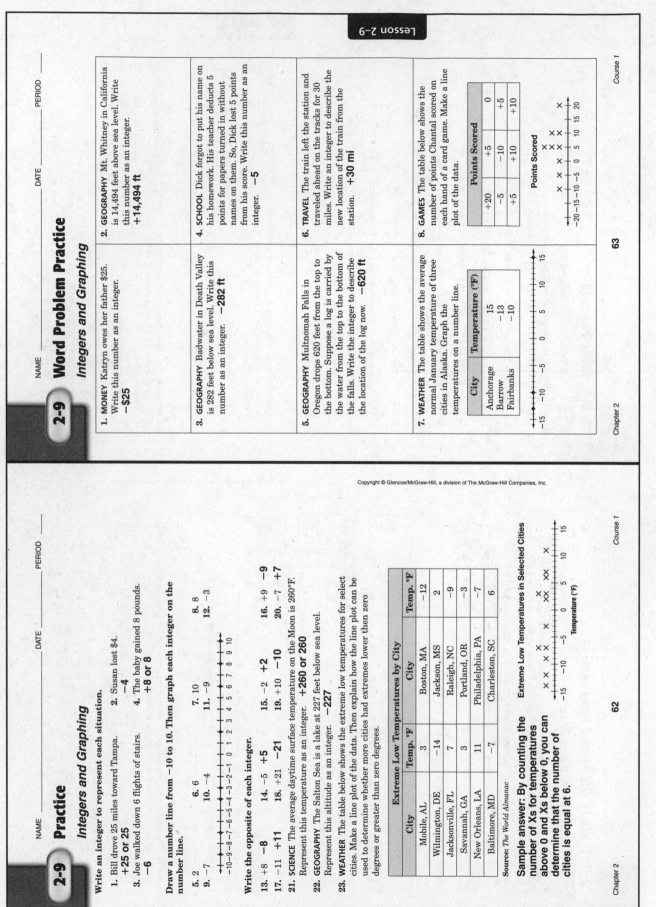

2-9 Word Problem Practice
Integers and Graphing

1. MONEY Katryn owes her father $25. Write this number as an integer. **-$25**

2. GEOGRAPHY Mt. Whitney in California is 14,494 feet above sea level. Write this number as an integer. **+14,494 ft**

3. GEOGRAPHY Badwater in Death Valley is 282 feet below sea level. Write this number as an integer. **-282 ft**

4. SCHOOL Dick forgot to put his name on his homework. His teacher deducts 5 points for papers turned in without names on them. So, Dick lost 5 points from his score. Write this number as an integer. **-5**

5. GEOGRAPHY Multnomah Falls in Oregon drops 620 feet from the top to the bottom. Suppose a log is carried by the water from the top to the bottom of the falls. Write the integer to describe the location of the log now. **-620 ft**

6. TRAVEL The train left the station and traveled ahead on the tracks for 30 miles. Write an integer to describe the new location of the train from the station. **+30 mi**

7. WEATHER The table shows the average normal January temperature of three cities in Alaska. Graph the temperatures on a number line.

City	Temperature (°F)
Anchorage	15
Barrow	-13
Fairbanks	-10

8. GAMES The table below shows the number of points Chantal scored on each hand of a card game. Make a line plot of the data.

Points Scored

+20	+5	0
-5	-10	+5
+5	+10	+10

Points Scored

2-9 Practice
Integers and Graphing

Write an integer to represent each situation.

1. Bill drove 25 miles toward Tampa. **+25 or 25**
2. Susan lost $4. **-4**
3. Joe walked down 6 flights of stairs. **-6**
4. The baby gained 8 pounds. **+8 or 8**

Draw a number line from -10 to 10. Then graph each integer on the number line.

5. 2   6. 6   7. 10   8. 8
9. -7   10. -4   11. -9   12. -3

Write the opposite of each integer.

13. +8 **-8**   14. -5 **+5**   15. -2 **+2**   16. +9 **-9**
17. -11 **+11**   18. +21 **-21**   19. +10 **-10**   20. -7 **+7**

21. **SCIENCE** The average daytime surface temperature on the Moon is 260°F. Represent this temperature as an integer. **+260 or 260**

22. **GEOGRAPHY** The Salton Sea is a lake at 227 feet below sea level. Represent this altitude as an integer. **-227**

23. **WEATHER** The table below shows the extreme low temperatures for select cities. Make a line plot of the data. Then explain how the line plot can be used to determine whether more cities had extremes lower then zero degrees or greater than zero degrees.

Extreme Low Temperatures by City

City	Temp. °F	City	Temp. °F
Mobile, AL	3	Boston, MA	-12
Wilmington, DE	-14	Jackson, MS	2
Jacksonville, FL	7	Raleigh, NC	-9
Savannah, GA	3	Portland, OR	-3
New Orleans, LA	11	Philadelphia, PA	-7
Baltimore, MD	-7	Charleston, SC	6

Source: *The World Almanac*

Extreme Low Temperatures in Selected Cities

Sample answer: By counting the number of Xs for temperatures above 0 and Xs below 0, you can determine that the number of cities is equal at 6.

NAME _____ DATE _____ PERIOD _____

2-9 Enrichment

Graphs with Integers

Statistical graphs that display temperatures, elevations, and similar data often involve negative quantities. On graphs like these, the scale usually will have a zero point and will include both positive and negative numbers.

For Exercises 1–6, use the bar graph at the right to answer each question.

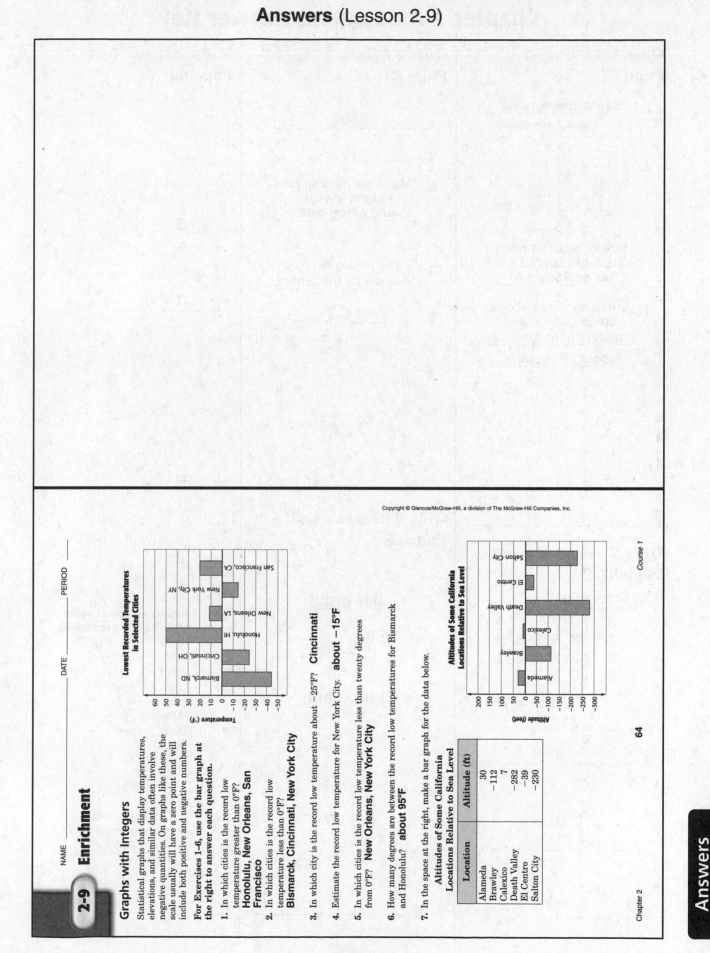

Lowest Recorded Temperatures in Selected Cities

1. In which cities is the record low temperature greater than 0°F?
   Honolulu, New Orleans, San Francisco

2. In which cities is the record low temperature less than 0°F?
   Bismarck, Cincinnati, New York City

3. In which city is the record low temperature about −25°F? **Cincinnati**

4. Estimate the record low temperature for New York City. **about −15°F**

5. In which cities is the record low temperature less than twenty degrees from 0°F? **New Orleans, New York City**

6. How many degrees are between the record low temperatures for Bismarck and Honolulu? **about 95°F**

7. In the space at the right, make a bar graph for the data below.

Altitudes of Some California Locations Relative to Sea Level

Location	Altitude (ft)
Alameda	30
Brawley	−112
Calexico	7
Death Valley	−282
El Centro	−39
Salton City	−230

Altitudes of Some California Locations Relative to Sea Level

Answers

Chapter 2 Assessment Answer Key

Quiz 1 (2-1 through 2-3)
Page 67

1. See students' work

2. **Students' Math Scores**

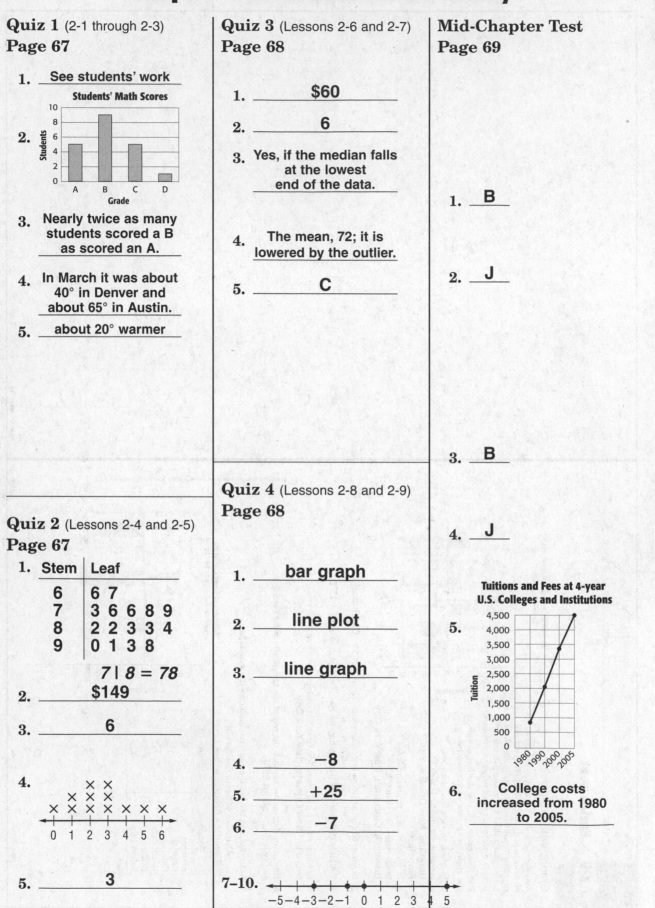

3. Nearly twice as many students scored a B as scored an A.

4. In March it was about 40° in Denver and about 65° in Austin.

5. about 20° warmer

Quiz 2 (Lessons 2-4 and 2-5)
Page 67

1.

Stem	Leaf
6	6 7
7	3 6 6 8 9
8	2 2 3 3 4
9	0 1 3 8

$7 \mid 8 = 78$

2. $149

3. 6

4.

5. 3

Quiz 3 (Lessons 2-6 and 2-7)
Page 68

1. $60

2. 6

3. Yes, if the median falls at the lowest end of the data.

4. The mean, 72; it is lowered by the outlier.

5. C

Quiz 4 (Lessons 2-8 and 2-9)
Page 68

1. bar graph

2. line plot

3. line graph

4. −8

5. +25

6. −7

7–10.

Mid-Chapter Test
Page 69

1. B

2. J

3. B

4. J

5. **Tuitions and Fees at 4-year U.S. Colleges and Institutions**

6. College costs increased from 1980 to 2005.

Chapter 2 Assessment Answer Key

Vocabulary Test
Page 70

1. ___median___

2. ___bar graph___

3. ___stems___

4. ___vertical axis___

5. ___key___

6. ___outliers___

7. ___mode___

8. ___line graph___

9. ___stem-and-leaf plot___

10. ___Average___

11. ___the difference between the greatest value and the least value of a data set___

12. ___the sum of the pieces of data in a set divided by the number of pieces of data___

Form 1
Page 71

1. ___A___

2. ___H___

3. ___A___

4. ___G___

5. ___C___

6. ___H___

7. ___C___

8. ___J___

9. ___C___

Page 72

10. ___J___

11. ___A___

12. ___J___

13. ___C___

14. ___F___

15. ___C___

16. ___G___

17. ___C___

18. ___J___

B: ___See students' work.___

Answers

Chapter 2 Assessment Answer Key

Form 2A
Page 73

Page 74

9. __D__

1. __D__

1. __C__

10. __J__

2. __J__

2. __G__

11. __D__

12. __F__

3. __B__

13. __C__

3. __C__

14. __F__

4. __J__

15. __B__

4. __H__

16. __F__

5. __C__

17. __D__

5. __C__

18. __F__

6. __H__

6. __G__

19. __D__

7. __B__

7. __A__

8. __H__

20. __F__

8. __H__

B: __4, 4, and 7__

9. __A__

Chapter 2 Assessment Answer Key

Form 2B *(continued)*
Page 76

Form 2C
Page 77

Page 78

10. **G**

11. **C**

12. **F**

13. **C**

14. **G**

15. **B**

16. **J**

17. **B**

18. **J**

19. **B**

20. **H**

B: **3, 3, and 9**

1.

Votes		
Person	**Tally**	**Frequency**
Mia	|||	3
Ali	卌 ||	7
Ted	||||	4
Hattie	卌		6

2. **Ali**

3. **Best Costume**

4. **Hattie had 3 more votes than Mia.**

5. **$49**

6. **$14; the outlier makes the mean higher.**

7. **Sample answer: mode; yes, because the mode is at the low end of the data set**

8.

Stem	Leaf
6	6 8
7	2 3 9 9
8	1 5 7 7 7
9	0 1 2 5 6

8 | 5 = 85

9. **10**

10. **30**

11. **86; 87**

---

12. **Student's Weekly Allowance**

13. **$5**

E

14.

15. **February**

16. **Sample answer: about $300 in August; by extending the line on the graph**

17. **−10**

18.

19.

20. **line graph**

B: **Sample answer: 1, 2, 3, 4, 5, 6, 7, 8, 9**

Answers

Chapter 2 Assessment Answer Key

Form 2D
Page 79

Page 80

1.

Votes		
Person	Tally	Frequency
Miguel	||	2
Aki	|||||	6
Tansy	||||||	7
Hannah	|||||	5

2. **Aki**

3.
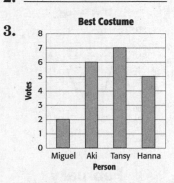
Best Costume

4. **Aki received three times more votes than Miguel did.**

5. **$33**

6. **$8; Since the outlier is greater than the other values, the mean is greater and not very representative of the data set.**

7. **Sample answer: mode; yes, because the mode is at the low end of the data set**

8.

Stem	Leaf
6	8 9
7	2 8 8 8
8	0 2 4 7 7 9
9	1 2 5 8

$8\ |\ 4 = 84$

9. **10**

10. **30**

11. **83; 78**

12.
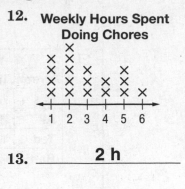
Weekly Hours Spent Doing Chores

13. **2 h**

14.
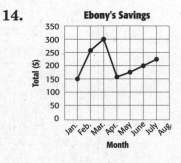
Ebony's Savings

15. **April**

16. **Sample answer: about $250 in August; by extending the line on the graph until reaching a vertical position of August**

17. **+25**

18.

19.

20. **bar graph**

B: **Sample answer: 1, 2, 3, 4, 5, 6, 7**

Chapter 2 Assessment Answer Key

Form 3
Page 81

Page 82

1. _____4_____

12. _____1990_____

2. _____14_____

13. _____1998_____

3. From the frequency able you cannot tell whether anyone scored 110 points.

14.
Stem	Leaf
11	0 8
12	0 0 5
13	
14	
15	5 6 6 6 9

12 | 0 = 120

4.

Annual Precipitation

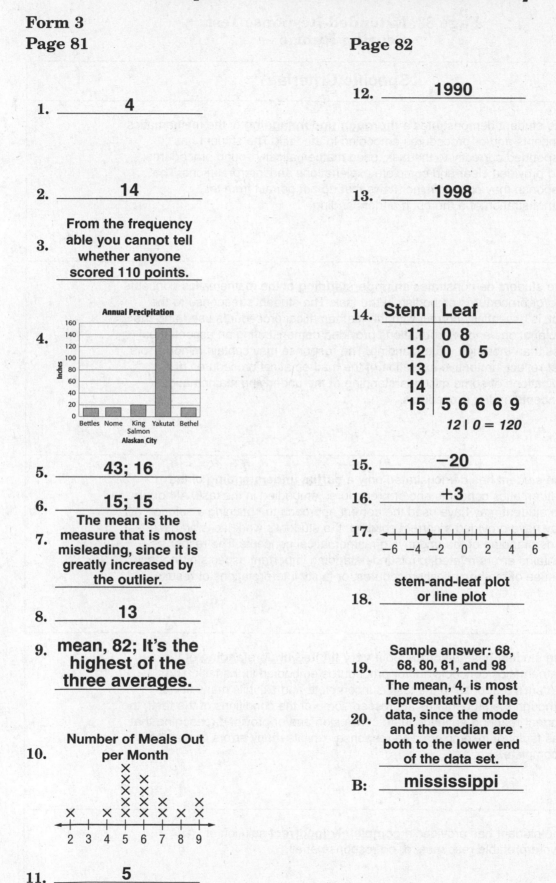

5. _____43; 16_____

15. _____−20_____

6. _____15; 15_____

16. _____+3_____

7. The mean is the measure that is most misleading, since it is greatly increased by the outlier.

17.

stem-and-leaf plot
or line plot

18.

8. _____13_____

9. mean, 82; It's the highest of the three averages.

19. Sample answer: 68, 68, 80, 81, and 98

20. The mean, 4, is most representative of the data, since the mode and the median are both to the lower end of the data set.

10. **Number of Meals Out per Month**

B: _____mississippi_____

11. _____5_____

Answers

Chapter 2 Assessment Answer Key

Page 83, Extended-Response Test
Scoring Rubric

Level	Specific Criteria
4	The student demonstrates a **thorough understanding** of the mathematics concepts and/or procedures embodied in the task. The student has responded correctly to the task, used mathematically sound procedures, and provided clear and complete explanations and interpretations. The response may contain minor flaws that do not detract from the demonstration of a thorough understanding.
3	The student demonstrates an **understanding** of the mathematics concepts and/or procedures embodied in the task. The student's response to the task is essentially correct with the mathematical procedures used and the explanations and interpretations provided demonstrating an essential but less than thorough understanding. The response may contain minor errors that reflect inattentive execution of the mathematical procedures or indications of some misunderstanding of the underlying mathematics concepts and/or procedures.
2	The student has demonstrated only a **partial understanding** of the mathematics concepts and/or procedures embodied in the task. Although the student may have used the correct approach to obtaining a solution or may have provided a correct solution, the student's work lacks an essential understanding of the underlying mathematical concepts. The response contains errors related to misunderstanding important aspects of the task, misuse of mathematical procedures, or faulty interpretations of results.
1	The student has demonstrated a **very limited understanding** of the mathematics concepts and/or procedures embodied in the task. The student's response to the task is incomplete and exhibits many flaws. Although the student has addressed some of the conditions of the task, the student reached an inadequate conclusion and/or provided reasoning that was faulty or incomplete. The response exhibits many errors or may be incomplete.
0	The student has provided a **completely incorrect** solution or uninterpretable response, or no response at all.

Chapter 2 Assessment Answer Key

Page 83, Extended-Response Test
Sample Answers

In addition to the scoring rubric found on page A36, the following sample answers may be used as guidance in evaluating open-ended assessment items.

1.

Students' Grades		
Grade	**Tally**	**Frequency**
A	||||	4
B	卌|	6
C	卌卌	10
D	||||	4
F	||	2

2. a.

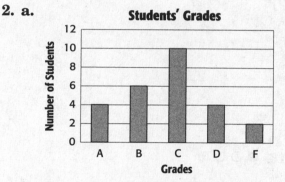

Students' Grades

b. The scale includes the number of students getting each grade. The interval is 2 in order to make all data fit easily on the graph.

c. The graph shows how many students got each grade. It compares the different grades.

d. The number of students with a grade of A is the same as the number with a grade of D. It is twice as many as the number of students with grade of F.

3. a.

Bicycle Sales

b. The scale is 0 to 25. The interval is 5. These were chosen to make the graph a manageable size.

c. The graph shows the change in sales of bicycles over a few years.

d. The sales went down slightly, went back up to where they started, then increased steadily at the same rate.

e. Bicycles sold should be about 25,000, which can be found by extending the line until reaching a vertical position of 2010.

4. a.

Stem	Leaf
3	4
4	
5	
6	6 8
7	2 6 6 6 8 8 8
8	0 2 2 2 2 4 4 6 8
9	0 2 4 4 8 $5|6 = 56$

b. The data is clustered between 66 and 98.

c. mean: 80; median: 82; mode: 82; range: 64

d. 34 is an outlier. Without the outlier, the mean is 82. The outlier brings the mean down.

Answers

Chapter 2 Assessment Answer Key

Standardized Test Practice

Page 84   **Page 85**

1. Ⓐ Ⓑ Ⓒ ●

                                    11. Ⓐ ● Ⓒ Ⓓ

2. Ⓕ ● Ⓗ Ⓙ

                                    12. Ⓕ Ⓖ ● Ⓙ

3. Ⓐ Ⓑ Ⓒ ●

4. ● Ⓖ Ⓗ Ⓙ

5. Ⓐ ● Ⓒ Ⓓ

                                    13. ● Ⓑ Ⓒ Ⓓ

6. Ⓕ Ⓖ ● Ⓙ

                                    14. _____**21**_____

7. Ⓐ ● Ⓒ Ⓓ

                                    15. _____**24**_____

8. Ⓕ ● Ⓗ Ⓙ

9. ● Ⓑ Ⓒ Ⓓ

10. Ⓕ Ⓖ Ⓗ ●

(continued on the next page)

Chapter 2 Assessment Answer Key

Standardized Test Practice *(continued)*
Page 86

16. _____16 children_____

17.

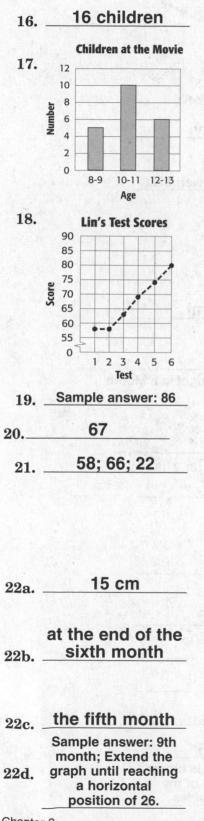

Children at the Movie

18.

Lin's Test Scores

19. _____Sample answer: 86_____

20. _____67_____

21. _____58; 66; 22_____

22a. _____15 cm_____

22b. _____at the end of the sixth month_____

22c. _____the fifth month_____

22d. Sample answer: 9th month; Extend the graph until reaching a horizontal position of 26.

Answers

Chapter 2 Assessment Answer Key

Unit 1 Test
Page 87

1. _____ **12 laps** _____

2. _____ **prime** _____

3. _____ **composite** _____

4. _____ **3 × 3 × 7** _____

5. _____ **2 × 2 × 3 × 3** _____

6. _____ **6^2; 36** _____

7. _____ **1^5; 1** _____

8. _____ **11** _____

9. _____ **15** _____

10. _____ **5** _____

11. _____ **41** _____

12. _____ **16** _____

13. _____ **14** _____

14. _____ **432 cm²** _____

15.

Math Score	Tally	Frequency
A	ⵌⵌ II	7
B	ⵌⵌ ⵌⵌ	10
C	III	3

16. _____ **B** _____

17.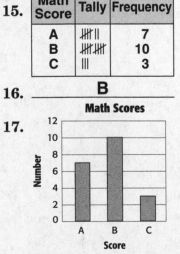
Math Scores

18. **More than three times as many students got a B as got a C.**

Page 88

19.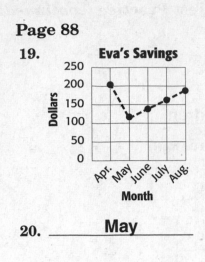
Eva's Savings

20. _____ **May** _____

21. _____ **Sample answer: $220** _____

22. _____ **15 mi** _____

23. _____ **3** _____

Lunches Bought in a Month

24.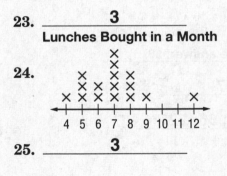

25. _____ **3** _____

26. _____ **7** _____

27. _____ **25** _____

28. _____ **4** _____

29. _____ **4** _____

30. _____ **2** _____

31. _____ **23** _____

32. **median; It is closer to more of the data values.**